Mountain Wilderness Survival

More books from AND/OR PRESS:

Along the Gringo Trail by Jack Epstein, an indispensable guide to budget travel in Latin America which goes beyond the usual tips on trains, buses and restaurants.

The Art & Adventure of Traveling Cheaply by Rick Berg, reveals the inside tips of extended budget travel throughout the world.

Hidden Hawaii: An Adventurer's Guide by Ray Riegert, the ultimate sourcebook for the secrets of this island paradise.

Vagabonding in the U.S.A. by Ed Buryn, an inside track to the best that America has to offer.

Hallucinogenic and Poisonous Mushroom Field Guide by Gary P. Menser, opens up the world of mycology in a clear and precise way.

Daily Planet Almanac edited by Terry Reim, an annual guide to celestial and planetary rhythms, gardening, horoscopes, tide tables, popular history, recipes, hints, charts and tales to inform, amuse and enlighten.

The Ecotopian Encyclopedia by Ernest Callenbach, a practical encyclopedia of simple living.

Mountain Wilderness Survival

by Craig E. Patterson

Foreword by Galen Rowell

Illustrated by Jeff Karl
with Vicki Klubok

And/Or Press, Inc.   **Berkeley, California**

Library of Congress Cataloging in Publication Data :

Patterson, Craig E.
  Mountain Wilderness Survival.

  Bibliography: pp. 187–188.
  Includes index.
  1. Wilderness Survival. I. Title.
GV200.5.P25   613.6'9   78-73379
ISBN 0-915904-39-X

Printed in the U.S.A.
First Printing April 1979

Published and Distributed by:
And/Or Press, Inc.
P.O. Box 2246
Berkeley, CA 94702

Developmental and manuscript editing: Ryan Garcia
Copy editing: Sayre Van Young
Typesetting: Richard Ellington
Proofreading: Marcia Bullard, Sayre Van Young
Indexing: Sayre Van Young
Photographs: Craig E. Patterson
Book design: Carlene Schnabel
Paste-up: Phil Gardner, Sandy Drooker

Dedication

To Dad, who introduced me to the outdoors, put me through school, and didn't hassle me when I gave up my hard-earned desk job to return to the outdoors.

Foreword

During World War II a Polish soldier named Slavomir Rawicz escaped from a Siberian prison camp and trekked over 4,000 miles to India, on foot the entire way. While crossing the Gobi Desert in August without animals or sufficient food, two of the seven members of his party died. On the twelfth of their thirteen days without liquids, Rawicz tried to remember if he had ever read how long a man could survive without food or water.

A conventional survival manual might have greatly lessened Rawicz's chances of survival. Most give the length of survival without water or other liquid as three to five days. Had Rawicz read this statistic in the middle of the desert, he might have given up hope. Trying to quantify survival is a little like trying to describe the beauty of the wilderness with numbers. Both attempts ignore the important emotional aspects.

Many people believe that survival lessons must be learned the hard way. An old proverb says, "Good judgment comes from experience; experience comes from bad judgment." This is not always true. It isn't necessary to freeze your fingers off or eat your best friend to gain survival knowledge. In fact, the most publicized survival success stories often have strong aspects of failure. A person who emerges relatively unscathed from an experience just doesn't have as interesting a story. For instance, the Donner Party perished from cold and hunger while nearby Indians, with far fewer material possessions, existed with no problems. In recent years a young man spent twenty-six days trying to find his way out of the wilderness in winter, starting out in good health, ending weak and frozen. He credited his *success* to his religious faith.

Craig Patterson has traveled the same area in winter where that young man nearly perished. His story has never been on the front pages of the newspapers because he knew what dangers he might encounter and he knew how to deal with them. He knew about shelters, food, clothing, and wild animals. And he had faith in his ability to read a map, a compass, and the stars to guide him over the best route.

Craig's survival guide is more like talking to an old Indian than a survivor of the Donner Party. He relies on common sense rather than firm rules. In a warm living room, rules sound just great. You read them and you plan not to break them. In the wilds, you have already broken them when you become aware of a problem. And the book you read emphasized the morality of not breaking rules rather than how to escape a situation outside the structure of approved actions.

Much of this book is anecdotal. It needs to be. We need to learn how our ancestors existed in the wilds for thousands of years. We do this best by example, not by cold facts. I learned most of my survival knowledge by being in the wilderness with top mountaineers who knew what they were doing. Not everyone is so lucky, but as far as written words are concerned, following Craig's footsteps through this book is as close as possible to walking and talking with him in person. We are led down a simple path, unencumbered by too much information coming too quickly.

My father was born in the Minnesota woods in 1884. When he went to college around the turn of the century, he was taught that human beings are incapable of original thought past the age of thirty. I've always laughed at that overstatement, but as I grow older (and past that deciding age), I realize there is an important kernel of truth behind the falsehood. Most of our thoughts come from past experience or knowledge. We do best what we have seen before. Creative solutions to problems always involve intense contemplation of things we already know. To improvise in the wilderness is to make something *already known* out of less than normal resources. Because we know about boats, we fashion a makeshift raft; because we know about hammocks, we fashion a bed in a tree out of rope. And because we know Craig Patterson's advice and experience, we will have the tools not only for survival but for finding enjoyment where the uninitiated find trouble.

Galen Rowell
Berkeley, California
December 1978

Acknowledgements

My special thanks to Rangers Jim Brady, Nancy Cushing, and Rick Smith for their astute comments about bears; to Susan Rossman for her typewriter and space; to Lynn Hammond for her efforts at polishing my rough prose; to Kathi Cursi for her long hours of typing. I would also like to thank my And/Or Press editors, Ryan Garcia and Sayre Van Young.

Table of Contents

List of Illustrations

Introduction

There's a character in the Li'l Abner comic strip who always had a black cloud looming over his head. That's me. Or at any rate, the two of us have a lot in common. Almost every time I go into the backcountry I get stormed on. My friends predict the weather by my trips: "Ah ha, must be a storm brewing! Craig's going on a three-day climb." Maybe I'm lucky in a perverse sort of way. Now whenever I go camping I always prepare for stormy weather regardless of how sunny the skies are when I leave. Less-experienced people (or those without my so-called "luck") go camping without adequate storm gear or enough food and when bad weather hits, they find themselves in life or death survival situations.

This book gives nuts and bolts tips on mountain survival. Much of the information comes from my own trial and error (mostly error) experiences and some, in part, from friends.

So how did I come upon all this Daniel Boone knowledge? Well, when I was about six I started "helping" my father on surveying trips through the woods. We lived in north-central Pennsylvania, an area surrounded by acres of rugged forest. By the time I was ten, I was going on my own excursions as an amateur naturalist looking for bugs, frogs, turtles, and snakes. In my teens I spent hours hunting animals and varmints and occasionally tried to talk my mom into raccoon rump roast for dinner. Many of my hunting days were actually spent stalking, exploring, and observing the natural phenomena of the forest and, along the way, learning how to stay alive and comfortable when that black cloud over my head started to spew forth raindrops or snow. As a kid I read every camping book I could get my hands on and listened carefully to any experienced outdoorsperson. Some of the best advice I ever got came from Ed McCarthy, a local hunting and river guide. He told

me the secret to safe and comfortable winter camping was "to
keep warm, keep dry, and keep your belly full." That advice
has echoed through my mind during miserable nights when I
didn't bring along enough food or warm clothes.

During all my hunting and backpacking trips I was occasionally lost or miserable for a few hours, but it wasn't until I took
up mountain climbing and white water canoeing that I experienced some really hazardous and scary situations.

While climbing volcanoes in Mexico, I learned about altitude
sickness and contaminated water. On an expedition to the
Cordillera Blanca in Peru (my black cloud loyally hovering
above) we counted the number of avalanches per hour, wondering if our camps were in a safe spot. Retreating from those
mountains, I backpacked into the Amazon basin and took a
thrilling swim in the Amazon River wondering if some water
creature might eat me in retribution for all the animals I'd
gobbled down. A trip to the Wyoming Rockies introduced me
to grizzly bears, lightning, and glacier crevasses. I've over-
turned in flood-swollen rivers and nearly met my maker on a
stormy Ontario lake. On various other trips I've suffered from
hypothermia, heat exhaustion, and poison ivy; I've fallen into
cracks, been pursued by bears, stung by sting rays, stuck in
quicksand, and chased by avalanches.

The point of this recital of perils is to let you know that the
mountain survival tips in this book have been well-tested. A
few of my partners have been killed in falls; others have been
incapacitated by stings, bites, sprains, breaks, frostbite, rockfall, sunburn, pulmonary edema, dysentery. So much for the
gruesome details. . . .

Right now I'm a forest ranger in Yosemite. I've completed
dozens of rescues on land, rock, and snow during every season
and in all weathers. Some of the people I've helped rescue were
unlucky victims of rockfall or sudden illness, but most of the
time they caused their own plight by climbing or hiking without proper equipment, taking short cuts without adequate
knowledge of the area—the list goes on.

Through my own mistakes and those of friends, I've learned
that good judgment is the key to mountain survival. Good
judgment means deciding to turn back before you get caught
out overnight in a storm. It means not crossing a stream, snow

slope, or cliff if conditions are adverse; remembering to bring matches, a raincoat, or flashlight if there's a chance you might need them. It means avoiding a dangerous situation rather than trying to deal with the consequences later. Although a lot of the information in this book might be new to you, the principle shouldn't be. A generation ago, humorist George Ade expressed it most succinctly: "An ounce of prevention is worth a pound of cure." This book explains the hazards and the prevention, but it must be combined with good judgment at the right time and place to do any good.

But above and *way* beyond all this fatherly "be careful" advice is my desire to enjoy and experience the wilderness and to have you do the same. Obviously I wouldn't put myself through all these hazardous experiences if there weren't something else out there—something magical, spiritual, special. It is something you will never find in a city—it's out there, it's yours; respect it and love it.

Chapter One:
Ready-to-Wear

Even if the only thought you usually give to your wardrobe is an occasional inspection of the expanding holes in your jeans, the clothes you wear in the mountains deserve more attention. Tennis shoes and shorts are fine on short warm weather hikes, but if you are lost or caught overnight in a storm, the clothes on your back, feet, and head can make the difference between comfort and misery, life and death.

Certain designs, fabrics, and insulating materials of various clothes are so superior to others that when the chips or you are down, you'll be glad (maybe for the first time in your life) you're wearing the *right* thing. Using a backpacking trip to wear out a raggedy old sweat shirt or socks with holes increases the risk of hypothermia, blisters, and frostbite. Resist wearing just any old thing, though some oldies like wool sweaters (without holes) are great. It all depends on what the item of clothing is made of and the conditions of your trip.

UNDERNEATH IT ALL

If I could stand it, I'd wear wool undergarments; wool is the only fabric that provides warmth even when wet (more on that later). But wool makes my skin break out in a rash, especially if I work up a sweat. Normally I wear cotton undergarments and use wool over them. If your skin can take wool, I'd advise wearing it instead of cotton for cold and wet weather travel. Or you could try wool–synthetic fabrics such as those made by Stil-Longs. They're fairly tolerable even to my sensitive skin, particularly after a couple of washings.

Cotton T-shirts and underpants are useful on a hot day when they'll wick perspiration away from your skin and has-

ten evaporative cooling. On a cold day they'll wick moisture
away from your skin into a protective layering of wool outer-
garments and keep you dry. Underwear that combines a 50/50
blend of cotton and polyester also provides both the desirable
wicking and quick-drying actions.

Nylon undergarments are the worst. If you wear them backpacking or on a ski tour, you'll be all wet. Synthetic fibers like
nylon, orlon, and fortrel have little ability to wick moisture
from one site to another. Although popular as quick-drying
fillers for sleeping bags and coats, they won't soak up perspiration if worn next to the skin.

In recent years the Scandinavians have developed polypro-
pylene undergarments that are now worn by most cross-
country ski racers. They wick moisture away from the skin,
are much warmer and lighter than cotton, and are non-scratchy
and better than wool in many regards. An excellent brand is
LIFA from Norway.

THE TOP HALF—SHIRTS, SWEATERS, JACKETS

The material of a shirt, sweater, or jacket is more crucial to
mountain survival than the design. In dry weather the material doesn't matter that much: a light down parka, a thick wool
or orlon sweater, even a thermal cotton sweat shirt will keep
you warm. But if you get caught in a rainstorm, the difference
between various materials will quickly become evident. The
down parka will become a sodden mass of lumpy feathers; the
warm loft will disappear along with your comfort. (See Chapter Two for more information on lumpy loft in sleeping bags.)
Since cotton absorbs water, the sweat shirt will get wet and
cold almost immediately. An orlon sweater won't absorb water
as quickly as cotton, but with enough exposure it will become
wet and provide only a fraction of its original insulation.

The wool sweater is the good guy here. Since wool tends to
shed water, the sweater will stay drier longer than other fabrics and will keep you warm. Even when a wool sweater or
jacket gets soaking wet, it's still the superior garment, especially compared to a cotton sweat shirt. The trouble with cotton is the wicking—evaporation cycle that occurs. It starts

inside the sweat shirt next to your skin. Liquid water absorbs heat from your cold and shivering body, evaporates and travels in the form of water vapor through the sweat shirt. Since cotton has very good wicking action, when the migrating water vapor condenses on the surface of the sweat shirt, it gets wicked back through the shirt to your skin. Again it is vaporized by body heat and the entire process starts again. Your body continuously loses heat to this back and forth cycle, and in the meantime you're not getting any drier or warmer. In fact, since the sweat shirt is robbing you of heat, you might be better off by removing it unless it's really windy.

Wool, the Good Guy

Since wool has relatively little wicking action, moisture that evaporates and condenses on the outside usually stays there instead of being wicked back in again. It's pretty easy to understand why wool garments are so highly recommended for cold or wet situations. Wet wool socks, pants, gloves, and shirts will always be warmer than other wet material. So when comparing the $6 price tag on a cotton sweat shirt to the $40 tag on a wool sweater think about what will happen if you get stuck in a rainstorm.

Acrylics

Orlon and other acrylics seem to fall somewhere between cotton and wool. Even though an acrylic sweater will get soaking wet quickly in rain and lose insulation value, it has no wicking action and dries quite fast, especially if you take it off, wring it out, and hang it in a sheltered place. The polyester pile jackets so popular with mountaineers will also dry quickly once out of the rain.

Stuffed Shirt

A thick layer of wool, down, or synthetic material around your body in cold weather is essential. If stuck out at night with just a light jacket or shirt, you can create a thick layer of insulation by stuffing any convenient dry material like leaves, crumpled paper, or grass inside your jacket. A jacket stuffed with pine needles can be just as warm as a down parka, though a little prickly.

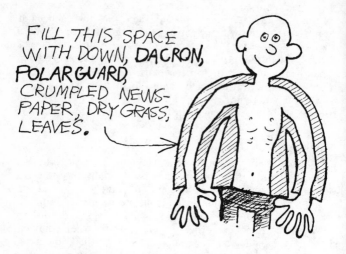

FILL THIS SPACE
WITH DOWN, DACRON,
POLARGUARD,
CRUMPLED NEWS-
PAPER, DRY GRASS,
LEAVES.

Fig. 1. Insulation—conventional or improvised—is essential for maintaining body warmth in cold weather.

THE LOWER HALF—PANTS, KNICKERS, SHORTS

The Trouble with Blue Jeans

Since jeans get wet easily, they're not particularly good for mountain survival. As soon as you kneel next to a stream for a drink of water or cross ski tips and fall into wet snow, your jeans will get damp. In cool weather they'll quickly begin to sap heat from your body. If drenched in a rainstorm, jeans are extremely uncomfortable and cold. When you get right down to it, jeans are probably one of the worst things to wear in foul weather. Even so, many Americans would sooner give up Mom, apple pie, and the Fourth of July than blue jeans. Every year thousands of jean-clad people go hiking, skiing, and camping in the snow. Jeans are the only pants some people will wear in the mountains (or any place for that matter), especially if they think downhill ski pants look plastic or that baggy wool knickers are too funky. If you refuse to give up jeans, then carry along some wool pants, wool long johns, or waterproof pants just in case, or consider wearing jeans made partially from a synthetic material like fortrel. They'll dry hours before all-cotton jeans and look just like the real thing.

Knickers

The combination of knickers and knicker socks allows max-imum freedom of movement and warmth if you're participat-ing in foul weather sports. By unfastening the knickers at the knees and rolling the socks down, you can cool off a lot faster in warm weather than if you were in long pants. Although wool knickers are best in cold wet weather, their weight and scratchiness make them undesirable for active cross-country skiing, especially on warm winter days. During strenuous per-iods of activity, I prefer to wear light nylon ski knickers that breathe and stretch as I move. If the temperature starts to drop, you can wear wool long johns under nylon knickers. During foul weather, try a pair of wind, rain, or powder pants over the knickers. The nylon one-piece knicker suits and bib knickers that are fast becoming popular for ski touring are very functional. Unlike regular knickers, they protect the small of the back from wind and snow.

Shorts

Hiking shorts are good on sunny days; they're cool and al-low extra freedom of movement. The cotton or cotton–syn-thetic blends are durable and will wick perspiration away from your skin. Remember to carry three essential items when you wear shorts in the backcountry: a pair of long pants in case of cold weather, insect repellent for your legs as well as the rest of you, and sunscreening lotion.

HEADGEAR

The type of hat you wear in the mountains depends on where you are and what you need protection from—sun, rain, or snow. A backpacker who has worked up a sweat might use a cotton bandanna to absorb perspiration; a bald backpacker might wear a beret for protection from the sun. One of my functional pieces of headgear is a tennis visor. On hot, sunny ski tours it shades my eyes from direct and reflected sunlight and acts as a sweatband, yet allows ample ventilation. During foul weather it keeps rain and snow off my glasses; used with a knit cap or hood it keeps my head warm and dry. Some people prefer felt crusher hats, brimmed cotton sunhats, or baseball caps.

If I could take just one hat into the backcountry, it would be a wool balaclava, a knit cap with a small visor, a face opening, and a knit extension for the neck. The design makes it possible for just your ears and the top part of your head to be covered if the weather's reasonable. If the weather gets worse, your neck and most of your face can be covered. A balaclava can even be worn while you sleep if it's really cold. Since the head is the major area of heat loss, always keep it warm.

HANDS UP

In general, mitts are warmer than gloves. Thick ragg wool or Dachstein mitts are probably the best for keeping your hands warm during miserable weather. The natural oil in these wool mitts sheds moisture well. They're about the only thing that will keep your hands warm during and after digging a cave in wet snow. Even wool socks on your hands will work if you don't have any mitts or gloves.

A wool glove worn under a nylon, leather-palmed overmitt is warm, versatile, and durable, but leather freezes easily if it gets wet. Down mitts are very warm because of the thick dead air space they provide, but they have to be kept dry. Cotton gloves are inexpensive and durable; they're also totally worthless when wet. Rubber or waterproof gloves can be useful, but if you're working in the rain or snow with your hands, the insides of the gloves will eventually get wet from perspiration and water will trickle around your wrists.

If your mitts become too slippery to grip equipment like an ice ax or rifle stock, coat the palms with plastic rubber (sold in most hardware stores) or coat the wooden surface of whatever you're trying to grip with pine tar or cross-country skier's hard wax.

On a cold day wet gloves will start to freeze as soon as you take them off. If you want to put them on later after lunch or rewaxing skis, don't hang them on the end of your ski poles like a lot of people do. Instead, put them inside your jacket so they'll stay warm and supple.

IF THE SHOE FITS

One of my favorite ways to size up strangers is to check out what they've got on their feet. Shoes make it easy to distinguish a rookie outdoorsperson from a veteran. Gucci loafers or platform shoes in the mountains say a lot about a person.

There's no one right shoe for the mountains. It all depends on what you're doing and where you are. A stiff-soled heavy leather boot is desirable for vertical ice climbing. A lightweight flexible boot is good for ski touring. Vibram-soled boots are ideal for mountaineering. Summer backpackers could wear a comfortable pair of crepe-soled moccasin work boots or even tennis shoes.

Backpackers are sometimes seen sitting along the trail nursing a heat rash and blisters caused by stiff "Super Mountain Boots" that arrived in the mail a week earlier. Always buy boots in person from a reputable shop that will make sure you get a correct fit, not a guess-fit through the mail. And consider what kind of terrain you'll be traveling in—wet, dry, warm, cold, on-trail, off-trail, snow, rock, or any combination of these.

Lightweight Boots

A common misconception is that boots have to be big and heavy to be warm. In truth, a flexible lightweight boot can be very warm as long as it's large enough to accommodate several pairs of socks to create thick dead air space. Make sure your toes can still wiggle with all those socks on. If the boot's too tight because of the socks, flexibility and blood circulation will be hindered. Cross-country skiers routinely stay out all day in freezing weather with nothing on their feet but skis, thick socks, and boots about as heavy and stiff as oxfords. The flexibility of their boots allows freedom of movement at the ball of the foot with each stride, thereby improving the circulation of warm blood throughout the foot.

Dry Feet

Socks get wet from sweat and from the water that seeps in from the outside. Waterproofing boots helps, but I don't know of a completely effective way to keep leather boots dry during prolonged exposure to water or wet snow. Sno-Seal is one of the most practical waterproofers available for mountain boots. It keeps them relatively dry through hours of continuous muck-sloshing. Liquid spray silicone waterproofers are easy to apply but they're expensive and don't protect as long as Sno-Seal. Also a boot waterproofed with Sno-Seal will look dry and lusterless when it needs to be waterproofed again; silicone-treated boots will only indicate this need by leaking. Although rubber boots are waterproof, sometimes accumulated perspiration makes them just as damp inside as the environment outside. Plastic bags worn over socks to keep out moisture have the same drawback.

Snowmobile boots (boots with felt liners, rubber bottoms, and breathable nylon or leather uppers) are excellent for cold wet weather. However, strapping them to snowshoes or crampons may decrease their insulating thickness and cause restricted blood circulation. In any case, carrying extra pairs of socks along to exchange for wet ones is about the easiest and most effective way to keep your feet warm.

Gaiter Aid

To prevent snow, water, rain, or gravel from getting into boots try wearing gaiters. They look like spats for mountaineers. Worn around the ankle and sometimes the calf, they also help insulate the lower leg, allowing warmth to spread down to the toes. Most mountaineers and skiers prefer breathable gaiters for subfreezing conditions and waterproof gaiters for heavy rain. In a survival situation either type will be better than no gaiters at all. You can tell the difference between breathable and waterproof fabric by holding the material tightly over your mouth with a cupped hand and trying to blow through it. If it's breathable, you'll feel your breath pass through the material and hit the palm of your hand. Air won't pass through waterproof material.

Insulate

To increase the thickness of insulation around the outside of a boot try some of these ideas. Winter mountaineers can use specially designed overboots to extend the temperature range of their mountain boots. Cross-country skiers can use nylon-rubber oversocks or synthetic-filled booties for touring boots. Skiers and snowshoers with small feet can make their own oversocks by cutting holes in the toes and heels of oversized ragg wool socks and pulling them over their boots. Even an extra 1/8-inch layer of insulation will make a tremendous difference in warmth.

Toasty Toes

The reason toes become so cold and numb is they're far from the body's warm central core and are the first body part to be denied full blood circulation. A good tip for toasty toes is to get your feet off the snow when you're not traveling. If you stand or sit on snow around a campfire your feet lose heat by conduction through your bootsoles into the snow. Insulate the bottoms of your feet by standing on skis, snowshoes, a bark slab, or a foam sleeping pad. Wiggle your toes around forcefully to get a little heat down there.

Put Your Hat On

Ever heard the expression, "If your feet are cold, put your hat on"? Well, it's true. In extremely cold weather, circulation to hands and feet is reduced because the body is conserving heat for the vital central core. Covering your head usually reduces radiation heat loss enough to alter the heat production balance and return circulation to your feet.

THE WET LOOK—RAINGEAR

The peaceful mood of a misty, rain-soaked forest is well worth experiencing as long as you're equipped with adequate raingear. But don't let the thermometer fool you. Paradoxically, it's easier to keep dry and warm traveling in a storm at temperatures around zero than when it's 32°F.

At zero the snow is very dry and so cold it doesn't melt when it comes in contact with boots, pants, gloves, or parkas.

At near-freezing temperatures the snow is very damp and clothes get wet. There are three basic approaches to keeping clothes dry while traveling in rain or wet snow, each useful at different times.

1. Rubber boots and a poncho or cagoule (pullover raincoat with hood) are good for repelling snow and water drops. But they don't allow body moisture to escape, so inside clothing gets wet from perspiration. Perspiration wetness is less of a problem if you're wearing a foamback cagoule or parka; these are especially effective in cold rain or wet snowstorms. During warm storms I've stripped to a T-shirt and shorts underneath a poncho, sweated throughout the day, then put my dry, warm clothes back on again after reaching my destination.

2. Another approach is to wear no raingear at all. During a seaside foraging trip on North Carolina's Cape Hatteras, I was defying June rains in rubber boots and a poncho while a friend combed the beach in nothing but trunks and sneakers. The wind was too chilly for me to try this, but he seemed comfortable enough and certainly had more freedom of movement than I did. Since then I've used a variation of this method while ski touring in snowstorms. Cagoules, parkas, and ponchos are uncomfortably restrictive, so when practical I wear wool socks, knickers, and enough wool sweaters to stay warm even while damp. This combination of clothes allows lots of flexibility, but at the end of the day I either have to get indoors or have a set of dry clothes to wear while I dry the others over a fire.

3. The third approach is to wear an outer waterproof garment that allows body moisture to breathe through the fabric. Clothes made of ventile cotton accomplish this because the fibers expand when wet, blocking the rain from penetrating further. Unfortunately, this type of cotton isn't 100 per cent effective. During steady rain the clothes underneath become soaked. Another drawback is that if the temperature drops after the storm, damp ventile will freeze solid. Gore-Tex, a more recently developed fabric, is both breathable and waterproof. Unfortunately Gore-Tex costs about one-third to one-half more than other more conventional waterproof materials. Unless you have a special need for Gore-Tex, it's easier on the budget to use cheaper, waterproof, nonbreathable equipment.

A precaution you should take with any waterproof garment is to seal the seams. Water will inevitably leak along the stitching lines unless they've been sealed with commercially-available sealing compounds such as Seam-Sealer or Rain Coat.

Chapter Two:
Gimme Shelter

When Mother Nature turns a cold shoulder on us, we need to cover our ass, so to speak, and just about everything else. Whether you're holed up in a snow cave or a luxurious penthouse, the principle in staying warm and dry is the same—thermal insulation.

Thermal insulation restricts heat transfer between mediums of different temperature. Despite modern technology, we've yet to find a more practical way to insulate our bodies than the method used by Stone Age people who wrapped themselves in bearskins—trapping dead air.

Fiberglass house insulation is a modern application of the dead air method. An uninsulated house has an empty space between the inner and outer walls. During cold weather, air in this empty space sinks after it contacts the cold outer wall. Then the air rises after it contacts the warm inner wall. Then it sinks again upon contact with the outer wall. As a result an air current exists within the walls transferring heat to the outside. Fiberglass insulation gets in the way of these air currents, producing still, dead air and a reduction in heat loss.

The insulating material isn't that important: fiberglass, styrofoam, ensolite, wool, down, dacron, and Polarguard are all good. The major factor in insulation is thickness: the thicker the layer of dead air, the more warmth.

A lot of people argue that goose down is warmer than duck down or warmer than dacron and so on. The reverse could be true depending upon the thickness. If the thickness is the same, then the insulating ability will also be about the same. Three inches of goose down, duck down, dacron, or even popcorn will all produce about the same insulating effect. The principle of insulation is important in selecting and preparing a warm shelter whether it's a tent, snow cave, or trench.

MAN-MADE SHELTERS

Selecting the Site

Below timberline is the best place to camp for the night: you're protected from the wind and useful construction materials like bark slabs, branches, and pine boughs are available. Another consideration in selecting a site is the microclimate. In brief, a microclimate exists on slopes with differing exposures to sunlight and wind. (See Chapter Seven for more information on microclimates.) Mountainsides that face north tend to be damper, cooler, and snowier than south-facing slopes. Ridge tops are often arid and windswept while valley bottoms are more moist and protected from strong winds. However, during calm weather at night, valley bottoms often channel a river of cold air from the high snowfields down to the foothills. Lake basins tend to trap these cold air flows. As a result lakeshore campsites can be many degrees cooler than a spot a few hundred feet higher on the mountainside. During a hot dry spell, you might prefer a site at the base of a mountain's shady north face close to the valley floor. During cold weather, you'd be warmer on a south-facing slope below the windy ridges.

Tents

Manufacturers now provide an amazing array of tents, each with special features that supposedly make that tent better than all the others. Even the fussiest equipment-hound should be able to find a satisfactory tent among the hundreds of models available.

The traditional A-frame tents (like the old Army pup tents) and the arched Quonset hut tents are still popular and functional for two or three people to sleep in. Wall and dome tents are normally designed for four to six people, or three to five people and a dog. The catenary curve tent (see illustration page 39) is presently considered the best wind resister according to backpacking experts. The droop or swayback tents are made of pieces of fabric sewn together and catenary cut along the seams. The effort involved in cutting and sewing all the pieces makes these tents very expensive. One model is $420! Unless you plan to camp on a windy ridge high in the Himalayas, you don't really need a tent that expensive. If you're camping in Wyoming in August, a Sears $35 canvas A-frame and a $12 waterproof tarp to protect it would probably be sufficient. The trend in tents today is towards the free-standing models that don't require stakes or guide lines. You can pitch them in soft snow with minimal effort and they can be moved to a new location when the snow melts simply by lifting them up, rather than restaking and repitching them. Every major supplier now carries these free-standing models.

The fabric of a tent should be woven tightly enough to shut out the wind and maintain still air space inside, but be porous enough to allow water vapor from cooking, breathing, and sweating to escape. Plastic tube tents are popular because they're waterproof and cheap, but they're not porous. When you close them to keep out wind and rain, water vapor condenses and drips inside, sometimes dampening equipment and/or campers. Canvas tents are inexpensive but somewhat heavy and susceptible to mildew and rot if wet when stored. Also if you brush a canvas tent during a rainstorm, the waterproofing action at that spot is destroyed.

Woven nylon tents are expensive but popular with mountaineers because they're light, strong, and mildew resistant. Most nylon tents are designed for the addition of a waterproof roof or fly that helps hold dead air space around the tent. This roof also helps prevent frost formation inside the tent. Gore-Tex tents are lighter than nylon tents with a roof or fly, but the lack of trapped outer air space makes them more susceptible to accumulated frost inside during freezing weather.

Waterproofing Tents

Any tent should be seam-sealed. Seepage can also be reduced by using a tent fly large enough to protect the tent and the ground surrounding it by several inches. On well-designed tents the waterproof fabric of the floor extends about six inches up the wall to prevent leakage from wind-driven raindrops that splatter onto the lower walls. If a tent doesn't have this feature, treat the lower walls with a silicone waterproofer. If you haven't sealed the seams or if the tent doesn't have a waterproof floor, pitch it on a high spot so pools and rivulets will drain away. You might also have to dig a trench three to four inches deep around the uphill sides of the tent. Since

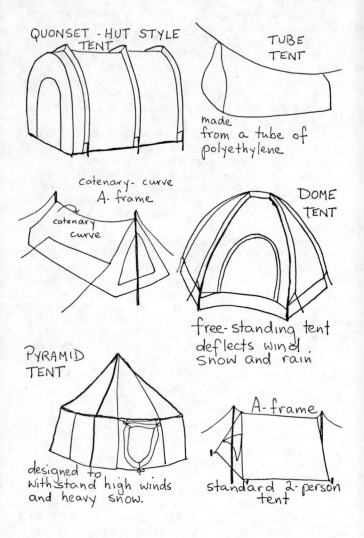

QUONSET - HUT STYLE TENT

TUBE TENT

made from a tube of polyethylene

catenary- curve A- frame

catenary curve

DOME TENT

free-standing tent deflects wind, snow and rain

PYRAMID TENT

designed to withstand high winds and heavy snow.

A- frame

standard 2-person tent

Fig. 2. Various tent designs are available to provide portable shelter.

PITCHING A TENT WITH RESPECT TO WIND

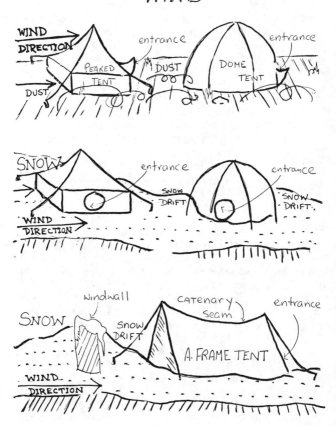

Fig. 3. How to pitch a tent with respect to wind conditions.

these ditches are extremely destructive to the forest floor they
should be avoided whenever possible by taking advantage of
natural drainage spots. If you must dig trenches, refill them
when you break camp.

Pitching Tents

In typical mountain soil, it's often difficult to drive a tent
stake into the rocky ground. A more practical method is to
anchor the tent guy lines to rocks and trees. On most backpacking trips I don't even bother to carry stakes. In the summer I use rocks and trees for anchors and in the winter I use
skis, poles, snowshoes, deadman anchors, crampons, pots, or
an X-shaped arrangement of sticks buried in the snow.

If you have to pitch a tent during a storm or in an area
where one might occur, a tiny clearing in the forest is the best
location. During most storms there's no locally predominant
wind direction on lower slopes so the tent should preferably
be pitched in a site sheltered from all directions. Avoid pitching the tent under trees; they drip for a long time after a rain,
and during a snowstorm they might drop heavy snow bombs
on your tent. If a snowstorm goes on for quite a while, periodically tighten guy lines and clear accumulated snow off the
tent to prevent the poles from collapsing and to protect you
from suffocation.

In windy locations pitch the tent so the door is facing downwind unless you're camping in snow when drifts could form
around the door. Pitch domed or tepee-shaped tents with the
doors sideways to the wind to keep it clear of snowdrifts. Pitch
the long axis of an A-frame or Quonset hut tent parallel to the
wind with the entrance downwind so the narrowest part of the
tent is exposed to the direct wind. If you have the time and
energy you could build a windwall upwind, three to four feet
high, but no closer than six feet to the tent. Since a windwall
slows down the wind, allowing snow particles to drop and form
a drift in the lee of the wall, the drift could form on top of
your tent if the windwall is too close.

Tarps

A tarp shelter can be made from a large (12-foot square)
piece of canvas, waterproof nylon, or plastic. A tarp is so light
that many backpackers carry one during the summer instead of

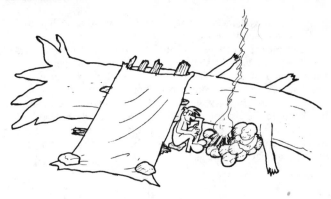

Fig. 4. An improvised shelter can easily be constructed by spreading a tarp over a framework of branches.

a tent in case the weather gets so bad they can't sleep outside. Tarps can be set up in numerous ways: A-frame, pup tent, lean-to, or any style you might invent on the spot. In an emergency, wrap the tarp around you.

If you want to anchor the tarp with guy lines but don't have any grommets, tie the guy line to a bulge in the tarp formed by wrapping it around a small rock. This method is actually stronger than grommet attachment if you have a plastic tarp. You can also lay a tarp over a framework of branches and anchor it by putting more branches on top. Insulate the top by adding an additional layer of grass or pine boughs.

Car Camping

Cars don't normally fall into the category of survival shelters, but they have proven to be lifesavers. A classic example occurred during a North Dakota blizzard several years ago. Drifting snow stranded two women in their car on a remote highway. One woman left the car to find help while the other remained inside. The woman in the car was rescued the next day, cold but alive. The other woman's frozen body was later discovered in a snowdrift. The moral to this tragic story is be prepared: equip your car with some newspapers (for insulation), blankets, candy bars, and water. *And* stay in the car if stranded under adverse conditions.

Since a car is both waterproof and windproof it can be an excellent foul weather shelter. If you have newspapers handy, hang them around the windows for insulation. Newspapers are a fair substitute for blankets too, as any park bench bum can tell you. You probably won't need a fire outside the car, but if it becomes necessary a matchless fire can easily be started by sparking a wire at the battery terminals onto some seat-stuffing soaked in gasoline. Also motor oil added to the fire will produce thick black smoke signals.

NATURAL SHELTERS

Boulder Caves and Rock Overhangs

These are the only really waterproof shelters Nature provides. I've used them at altitudes from sea level to fifteen thousand feet in North and South America. The caves in the Teton's upper Garnet Canyon (actually alcoves under piles of boulders) have kept me dry through ferocious rainstorms. In Yosemite

Fig. 5. Boulder caves and rock overhangs provide waterproof shelters for rainy nights.

Valley the Indian Caves (just recesses under large boulders) are such good shelters they were once used as seasonal homes by Native Americans. Large concavities in the sedimentary rock cliffs of Appalachian Mountain river gorges have sheltered many a camper during rainy nights. Abundant along the desert red rock canyons of Utah are immense overhangs, some large enough to accommodate several troops of Boy Scouts. In that event you might prefer to sleep out in the rain!

If a storm starts to brew, inspect nearby cliffs and boulders for possible hide-outs. A boulder cave, cliff overhang, or just an overhanging boulder wall can be used in conjunction with a lean-to made from branches, bark, grass, or a tarp. Sometimes you have to remove rocks for a smooth sleeping area, but they can be used to build a windwall. If you're going to sit out a thunderstorm in a boulder cave, choose a cave low on the mountainside even if it means abandoning another suitable shelter higher up. Boulder caves on high ridges or summits can be very dangerous if lightning is present.

I've never had to give up a shelter because it turned out to be an animal's home, but always consider the possibility that anything from bees to bears might live there. If you see bones, animal feces, and trodden ground in a cave, you can be pretty sure it's used by some type of animal. It'd be safer to find another shelter, especially if you're in grizzly country. Be cautious when you crawl under a boulder. Sometimes they're inhabited by rattlesnakes and scorpions.

If you make a fire in a boulder shelter, build it four or five feet away from the rock; then build a reflector wall behind the fire and sit between the fire and the boulder so heat reflects from both sides.

When the lip of an overhanging rock isn't particularly sharp, rain can trickle across the top, along the ceiling, and then drip on the people inside. Usually there's a telltale streak of lichen on the ceiling of a rock overhang where dribbles occur. If you see this line, don't sleep under it.

Fallen Logs

If you can't find a boulder shelter, fallen logs are a good second choice. They might be scarce in regularly logged forest, but uncut wilderness areas are full of potential log shelters. Try to find a log at least two feet in diameter to sit beside or

Fig. 6. Fallen trees are often good potential shelters.

underneath after building a roof and walls from branches and
bark slabs or snow blocks. If you build a fire in a log shelter
during the winter, be sure to knock the snow off the top so it
won't melt all over you. Deep snow areas in the Rockies and
the West Coast sometimes have useful shelters under sections
of logs that are raised a few feet off the ground but buried under snow. You can spot these hollow spaces by probing along
the edge of the log with a stick or ski pole. If you're lucky
enough to discover one, you'll have a blizzard-proof shelter
that only needs a bark slab and pine bough bed to be complete.

Tree Clusters

   Dense groupings of trees, preferably evergreens, provide
quick shelters from wind and snow, but they won't keep you
dry in a heavy rain. Although this type of shelter is a little
leaky, there's always a good supply of firewood on hand. And
if it isn't storming you'll be warmer under the trees because the
tree canopy protects against radiant heat loss to the black evening sky.

SNOW SHELTERS

If it's forty degrees outside, then the thirty-two degree temperature inside a snow shelter will seem very cold. But when it's ten below zero outside, that thirty-two degrees will be a welcome relief. Snow shelters have all sorts of advantages. Radiation heat loss is minimized because the white walls reflect heat just like Space Blankets. Emitted body heat is reflected back towards the body. When you lie on foam pads, bark slabs, pine boughs, empty water bottles, or any non-metallic equipment, conduction heat loss can be reduced to nothing through insulation. Convection heat loss is practically nil because there isn't any wind inside a snow shelter; evaporation loss will decrease as the still air is warmed and moistened from your breath. (These four varieties of heat loss are explained in detail in Chapter Four.)

If you grew up in the land of eternal sunshine and never were lucky enough as a kid (some people might not look at it this way) to spend hours building snow forts, snowballs, and tunnels, then you might need a little practice before you get a feel for the varying strength and cohesiveness of different types of snow. It wouldn't hurt to take a weekend trip to practice building snow shelters.

There are many types of snow shelters. Your choice will be determined mainly by snow conditions and the available digging tools. You need a fairly good-sized shovel to dig a snow cave; smaller snow shelters, especially those made with trees and logs, can be built using a lightweight aluminum shovel, a special snow saw, or even a cookie sheet to cut snow blocks. If you don't have a shovel, use snowshoes, pots, pans, spare ski tips, or metal cups. Always wear a raincoat and rainpants when building a snow shelter so you won't get wet.

Snow Blocks

Cookie sheets cut nice snow blocks, but skis are also quite efficient. To use them, draw a block on the surface of the snow, then cut it out by stabbing the tail of the ski straight into the snow along the lines. Before you lift the block out of the snow, reslide the ski tail along each side to make sure the cut is complete. To break the block loose, slide your fingers into the cut on one side and push against the wall until it de-

Figs. 7 & 8. To prepare snow blocks for building various shelters: draw block outline on snow surface; then cut block out, using snow shovel, cookie sheet, snowshoes, or skis. Lift block out carefully.

Fig. 9. Working together to build an igloo: one person cuts snow blocks and the other works inside the circle laying blocks in an inward-leaning spiral.

Fig. 10. A near-complete block house: walls have been built and skis and poles set up to support tarp for roof; snow blocks can be added to anchor the tarp and insulate the roof.

taches from the bottom and comes out. If you're using lightweight touring skis instead of heavy mountain skis, don't try
to break the block loose by levering the tail end of the ski.
The ski will probably break before the block comes out. Snow
blocks are excellent for building the various shelters discussed
in the following section.

Igloos

Although igloos make fine winter shelters, they're time-
consuming and difficult to build without prior experience. If
you've never made one and have only a few daylight hours left,
you'd be better off trying something easier.

The basic process in igloo building is to cut and lay a spiral-
ing inward-leaning series of snow blocks. In a group, generally
one person will work from inside the igloo setting up walls
while the others cut and carry blocks to the igloo. The heavier
the blocks the better since they fuse with each other, but don't
cut blocks so big the person inside the igloo can't lift them.
If you're in powder snow, pack it with skis or snowshoes and
leave it about half an hour so the snow can strengthen and become consolidated enough to cut. Warm, wet, thirty-two degree snow blocks don't freeze together very well. It's far easier
to build an igloo out of the type of bitter cold snow found in
the mountains of New Hampshire than the milder snow of the
Pacific Coast mountains.

Block Houses

These structures resemble modified igloos. Roomy and
windproof, they take only about half an hour to build. First
decide on a floor plan and draw it on the snow. Pile the blocks
along the lines to the desired height. The flat roof can be made
of ski poles, snowshoes, branches, or bark slabs. Cover everything with a tarp (if available), then a layer of snow blocks to
anchor the roof and insulate the shelter. One of the more common mistakes with block houses is making the walls too far
apart to cover with a tarp.

Snow Caves

During winter mountaineering expeditions with high cold
winds, snow caves are probably the most efficient shelter.
Some can be quite luxurious, almost like regular houses. One

time on an expedition to Mt. McKinley we built a split-level snow cave with a sleeping room, kitchen, and entrance alcove. We cut shelves into the walls for storage, and designed parabolic recesses to reflect candlelight into the rooms. Your snow cave needn't be this elaborate, but the floor plan and design is only limited by imagination and time. If you plan to stay in an area for only one night, it's more practical to pitch a tent than to build a snow cave.

Unfortunately there are usually a limited number of sites suitable for snow caves. For a roomy snow cave that isolates you from blizzards, a slope with snow depths of about eight feet is best. Except on extremely high mountains, deep snow is usually found only in snowdrifts on the lee of hills or ridges. Lee slopes are avalanche-prone and should be used only if the snow is stable. On the plus side, though, snow caves can be built above timberline, an area where most other types of shelters aren't feasible. Variations of the basic snow cave can be used in conjunction with fallen logs, boulders, or tree wells.

I usually carry two shovels to build snow caves—a short-handled, steel, round-nosed shovel to dig and chip inside the shelter and a large aluminum shovel (4½-pound grain scoop) to move snow from the entrance. Even with shovels a couple of hours are usually needed to build a simple liveable snow cave.

There are several basic principles to follow when building a snow cave:

1. If the snow is deep enough, build the cave on a steep slope so it will be easier to shovel away excavated snow from the entrance.

2. If possible, dig the entrance below the floor level so warm air inside can't escape. Where the terrain is too level, build the entrance at a convenient height and then seal it for the night with snow blocks or backpacks after you're inside.

3. The shape of the ceiling isn't critical when you're using very cold, hard, compact snow. But in softer, warmer snow, the roof must be domed properly or it will sag during the night. Sculpt the ceiling in the shape of a dome, like the end of an egg. Make it as high as the floor is wide. If the snow is wet, make the ceiling even higher than the width of the floor.

4. While you're excavating the inside of a snow cave, you

might start to notice a bluish-green light penetrating the roof
and walls from the outside. Don't dig any further in that direction. This light means that the walls are barely thick enough
to be stable. On the positive side, though, that light diffusing
through the walls means oxygen is permeating through, thereby eliminating the necessity of punching air holes.

5. Keep an eye out for a dwindling air supply, especially
during storms. You might notice that the candle flame is getting dimmer or that your breathing is becoming rapid and
shallow. If this happens, punch air holes in the walls. One
time during a storm, several feet of snow fell on top of our
cave during the night. Since we were asleep we didn't realize
what had happened. In the morning we woke up taking rapid,
shallow breaths and feeling unusually restless. When I tried to
light a candle the matches just fizzled and went out. After the
third fizzled match, I finally realized there wasn't enough oxygen and we were actually starting to suffocate. We quickly dug
a new airway through the walls which had become six feet
thick during the storm.

6. Carbon monoxide poisoning is a danger if you cook inside a snow cave (or inside any shelter, for that matter). Nausea and headache are the usual early warning signs, but not
always. You might not feel anything until it's too late. So be
sure to ventilate any shelter whenever there's a fire, stove, or
gas lantern burning inside.

7. If you know beforehand that you'll be sleeping in a
snow shelter, try to bring along some extra foam pads. You
need at least twice the amount of insulation underneath you
on snow than is required on dry ground.

Powder Snow Shelters

If the snow isn't deep enough to dig a cave, an alternative is
a powder snow shelter. You can build one on level ground with
a snow layer only two feet deep. Use shovels, snowshoes, or
whatever to heap the snow into a pile at least eight feet high
for a shelter that will be six feet wide, six feet high, and two
feet thick. If the snow is extremely powdery, tap it often with
a shovel while piling it up to speed consolidation. Once you've
built the pile, leave it for about half an hour to consolidate and
harden. Then dig out the interior of the pile as if it were a
snow cave. On level ground it won't be practical to try to con-

struct an entrance below the floor level. Make sure the ceiling is as high as the floor is wide and stop digging where light penetrates the walls. You could also build a quick, makeshift shelter by piling powder snow up next to something like a boulder, letting it harden, then digging a partial snow tunnel using the boulder as one wall.

Snow Trenches

Snow trenches can often be built in areas where no other type of shelter would be feasible: in just a few feet of snow, above or below timberline, on slopes or level ground. Shaped rather ominously like a grave, snow trenches can be lifesavers if you're caught on a mountain during a blizzard. To make one, outline the shape on the snow surface. Allow enough width for elbow room—three feet is usually enough for one person, five feet for two. Since it's hard to construct a roof across a wide trench, keep the width at snow surface narrow but make it wider inside as you dig down. The length should be six to eight feet so you can stretch out.

You can shovel soft powder snow out of the trench with snowshoes or stand alongside and sweep the snow out with the tail of your ski. Later inside the trench reach out with your

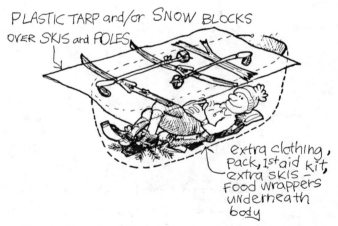

PLASTIC TARP and/or SNOW BLOCKS
OVER SKIS and POLES

extra clothing, pack, 1st aid kit, extra skis — food wrappers underneath body

Fig. 11. Home Sweet Home: a snow trench can provide a snug shelter.

ski held horizontally and bulldoze the snow off the surface towards the edge of the trench. Then mound the snow to increase the height of your walls. This allows you to dig a shallower trench with enough ceiling height to sit in the shelter. Harder snow can be removed by cutting it into blocks with skis or snowshoes. Place the blocks along the edges of the trench for more height or save them to build a roof.

The type of roof covering the trench will vary with snow conditions and equipment available. Above timberline you can make a strong roof from skis, poles, or snowshoes with a poncho spread over the top, then a layer of snow to anchor the poncho and insulate the shelter. You could also use snow blocks: either lay them over the ski and pole frame or place them in the shape of an A-frame—blocks on opposite sides leaning against each other—over the trench.

Above timberline you'll need to insulate the bottom of the trench. Use your equipment: climbing rope, spare cord, first-aid kit, plastic ski tips, etc. Or sit on your boots and put your feet inside your pack for warmth. Below timberline you can use bark slabs, pine boughs, or similar materials.

Fig. 12. A tree well offers numerous possibilities for shelter to the imaginative builder.

Tree Wells

In forests with deep snow (as you'll find in the Rockies, the Pacific Coast range, Canada, or Alaska), tree wells are natural phenomena. A tree well is a conical depression of hollow rings in the snow around a tree trunk (usually evergreen) that forms because the canopy of branches above protects the area from snowfall. A tree well can serve as a quick effective shelter in an emergency, and can, in general, offer numerous possibilities for an imaginative builder. You can lay a framework of branches, or skis and poles across the well; then cover them with a tarp, bark slabs, and/or snow. You can also make a partial block house or snow cave inside the well by tunneling into the snow away from the tree trunk. Occasionally the snow-covered tree branches extend all the way to the snow level, forming ready-made walls and roof. If this is the case, you only need to excavate a comfortable floor and add ground insulation like bark slabs or pine boughs for a bed.

SLEEPING BAGS

Most people need at least three inches of loft (the thickness of the bag) in subfreezing weather. If you're strictly a warm-weather camper, you won't need a bag with so much loft. Often you hear that dacron Fiberfill II (or Polarguard) sleeping bags aren't as warm as down bags. That's just because most commercially-made synthetic bags aren't as thick as down bags. If they were, they'd be about equal in warmth. Many manufacturers describe bag thickness in terms of *total* bag loft—top plus bottom layers—so in such cases halve the loft in order to estimate the dead air space. A synthetic bag will probably weigh one or two pounds more than goose down even when both are the same thickness. Also a synthetic bag will cost about two-thirds as much as a down bag.

If your bag stays dry, practically any type of filler will keep you warm, but some fillers stand up better than others when soaked in a storm. When down gets wet, the feathers collapse or mat, losing their ability to insulate. In contrast, wet synthetic fillers still retain most of their loft and much of their insulating value. If you're going on a boat or camping trip in rain country, take a synthetic bag or be prepared to keep your

Sleeping Bag Comparison Table

Brand and Model	Filler	Weight (in pounds)	Top Loft (dry, in inches)*	Price†
Alpine Products #1 Mummy	P	4¼	3½	$ 80
North Face "Bigfoot"	P	5 1/8	3½	$ 90
North Face "Superlight"	D	3 1/16	3½	$160
Sierra Designs "Cirrus"	D	3	3½	$280
REI "Monarch"	D	3¾	3½	$170
Alpine Products #3 Winter Mummy	P	5	5	$ 86
Sierra Designs "Nimbus"	D	4¼	5½	$425
North Face "North Face"	D	5¼	5	$305
REI "Denali"	D	5¾	5	$225

Filler: *D* Down, *P* Polarguard

*Unless manufacturer states otherwise, assume that top loft is half of total loft.
†Prices subject to change.

Note: Try to use a closed-cell foam pad underneath your sleeping bag; it won't sponge up water. In summer a ¼"-thick pad is enough for a rugged individual, but a 2"-thick pad might be necessary in the winter.

down bag dry. Always wrap your sleeping bag (down or synthetic) in a plastic trash bag to keep it dry while you're traveling. Don't wear wet clothes to bed. Evaporation will dampen the sleeping bag. Put wet clothes in a plastic bag inside or under your sleeping bag to keep them from freezing during the night. Some people put a waterproof liner inside their sleeping bag so body moisture can't escape into the down. This keeps the insulation dry but can also produce uncomfortably high humidity inside the liner.

The effectiveness of synthetic fillers was proven to me during an expeditionary ski tour through the St. Elias Mountains in Alaska. I was traveling on ice and snow for about a month, with nighttime temperatures always below freezing, and often below zero. Practically every morning frost was on my sleeping bag because of the moisture that had evaporated from my body during the night. The weather in the morning often made it impossible for me to dry the bag before breaking camp. So I stuffed it into my pack while it was still damp with frost. After several days of accumulated frost, the bag was noticeably damp when touched, but the insulating value hadn't been appreciably reduced. I was comfortable and warm every night with about a four-inch layer of synthetic filler (Snow Lion Polarguard). Under similar conditions on other expedition trips my damp down-filled sleeping bag collapsed partially, and I slept in some chilly beds.

The sleeping bag comparison table on page 54 lists some of the more popular brands and their qualities. Remember, you don't really need a five-pound bag if you're strictly a summer camper.

Chapter Three:
Incredible Edibles

Food always seems to taste better in the mountains. Maybe it's the fresh air, the extra effort involved in preparing it, or merely the fact that you always seem to be starving. At any rate, fresh-brewed coffee mingled with the scent of pine on a beautiful morning in the mountains is as good if not better than Mrs. Olson's kitchen-bound brew.

EAT YOUR BREAKFAST

Breakfast is the key to your strength during the day.* Fats and proteins eaten in the morning provide a steady supply of energy through the afternoon and evening. They also stabilize the rate at which the quick energy of sugar is burned. Large meals outside can make you uncomfortably chilly during digestion so try to eat inside or in warm sunshine. If the weather's too miserable to stop for a regular lunch, eat several quick snacks along the way so you won't get cold and travel slowly enough to allow for digestion. In brief, the concept is to nibble frequently rather than chow down huge amounts of food at one sitting.

Seeds, nuts, and animal meat provide more energy than green vegetation. Sugary foods are the quickest to be digested if you're cold; they require the least amount of water for digestion.† Fats provide about twice as much energy per pound as other foods but spoil easily. Good foods to carry for emer-

---

*USDA, *Food,* p. 323; and Adelle Davis, *Let's Eat Right to Keep Fit,* Chapter Two.

†Warren Bowman, M.D., *Mountain Medicine Symposium,* p. 14. "If there aren't enough fluids to drink . . . eat carbohydrates instead of protein or fat, since carbohydrate is broken down completely into carbon dioxide, water, and energy and does not produce either organic acids or nitrogenous byproducts."

Grocery List
Backpacking Foods Available at Supermarkets

- **Breakfast**
  Tang (with or without nutritional yeast mixed in)
  Dried fruit and nut mix
  Granola, bran flakes, farina, Quaker Instant Oatmeal
  Coffee, tea, hot chocolate (Hershey or Swiss Miss), Ovaltine

- **Lunch**

Nuts:	Almonds, beechnuts, Brazil nuts, cashews, filberts, macadamia nuts, peanuts, pecans, pine nuts, walnuts
Cheese:	Your favorite kind
Dried Fruit:	Apples, apricots, bananas, dates, figs, peaches, pears, pineapple, prunes, raisins
Luncheon Meat:	Bologna, braunschweiger, liverwurst, Spam, salami, thuringer, Vienna sausage (all will keep one day without refrigeration)
Dried Meat:	Beef jerky
Starch:	French bread rolls, Rye Crisp, Ritz crackers, Wheat Thins, buffet-style rye bread, pumpernickel bread
Drinks:	Water with Wylers or Kool-Aid, Gatorade, ERG, Body Punch

- **Dinner**

Soup:	Lipton's Cup-a-Soup
Main Course:	Meat-noodle combination—egg noodles with canned roast beef, corned beef, boned chicken, tuna, or turkey (add powdered cream of mushroom soup, onion, and cheese for flavoring); canned chicken chow mein or beef chow mein with noodles
Drinks:	Bouillon, coffee, tea, hot chocolate
Dessert:	Instant pudding, Jiffy popcorn

- **Staples**
  Salt and pepper
  Margarine or butter (weather permitting)
  Honey or sugar for cold weather travel
  Powdered milk

- **Rainy Day Morale Boosters**
  Peanut butter
  Marie biscuits
  Sardines, anchovies
  Dried sweetened pineapple chunks

gencies are Tootsie Rolls, Hershey bars, chocolate-covered nut bars, beef jerky, pemmican, dextrose tablets, raisins, Kendall mint cake, Wilson's Bacon Bar, and similar foods that won't get squashed.

STORE-BOUGHT FOOD

Always carry more food than you plan on using in case you get caught in a storm or are lost for a couple of days. You'll be able to sit tight without starving and wait for rescue or the storm to end. You don't have to rely on the special freeze-dried food sold in mountaineering supply stores. As you can see in the table on page 58, your favorite supermarket will have many foods suitable for backpacking in terms of weight, cost, perishability, and crushability. Don't forget special taste treats. If you're stuck in a tent on a rainy day, special snacks or a shot of brandy in a cup of tea can bring about a big improvement in morale and patience.

EDIBLE PLANTS

Edible plants are common in vegetated areas throughout North America, but because they contain minimal food energy and take a long time to be assimilated by the body, the extra energy burned running around picking berries is usually greater than the caloric value of the food. A person collecting plants in a rainstorm for one hour would probably metabolize three or four hundred calories. To come out even, you'd have to pick, wash, cook, eat, and digest over two pounds of dandelion greens or three pounds of wild onions in one hour! If you were stuck in the wilderness for weeks, the vitamins and minerals in these plants would be useful as long as you gathered them on sunny days when hypothermia wasn't a threat. However, if you were huddled under a boulder on a cold, snowy night, death from vitamin A deficiency would be the least of your worries. Conserving energy and staying warm is much more important. People can survive for weeks without food as long as they have water.

In the chance that wild plants could be useful for long term

SURVIVAL FOOD

	Calories per pound edible portion before cooking

- **Candy**

Chocolate-coated almonds	2581
Hard	1751
Milk chocolate	2359

- **Fish**

Bass, smallmouth or largemouth, flesh only	472
Bullhead, fillets	381
Carp, flesh only	522
Catfish, freshwater, fillets	467
Pike, Walleye, flesh only	422
Salmon, Chinook (king), flesh only	1007
Trout, Rainbow, flesh with skin	885

- **Meat, Fowl, and Shellfish**

Clams, meat only	363
Crab, saltwater, meat only	422
Crayfish, freshwater, meat only	327
Duck, wild, total edible portion	613
Eel, American, flesh only	1057
Eggs (duck, goose, turkey), average	700
Frog legs	215
Rabbit, wild, ready to cook	490
Snail (ugh!)	408
Turtle, green, muscle only	404
Venison, lean meat	572

- **Berries**

Blackberries	250
Blueberries	259
Currants	220
Elderberries	307
Gooseberries	177
Grapes, American type, fair quality	178
Raspberries, Black	321

- **Nuts**

Beechnuts, shelled	2576
Butternuts, shelled	2853
Hickory nuts, shelled	3053
Pine nuts, Piñon, shelled	2880
Walnuts, Black, shelled	2849

- **Other Plants**

Chicory greens	74
Dandelion greens	204
Mushrooms, edible species	154
Mustard greens	98
Onions, young, bunching varieties, bulb and entire top	157
Onions, bulb and white portion of top	76
Purslane leaves	95
Watercress leaves, including stems	79

survival situations, I'll mention a few of the most easily identifiable types found in unpopulated areas of North America. You might also want to get a plant guidebook for the area you'll be traveling in; learn to identify local edible *and* poisonous plants. Never eat any plant you can't positively identify as safe. Spit out parts that taste bitter; they might be poisonous. Also a lot of plants that animals can eat are toxic to humans. For instance, squirrels can eat raw acorns which are poisonous to us unless cooked.

Nuts

All cone-bearing pine trees and firs (genera *Pinus, Abies, Pseudotsuga)* yield edible nuts. Some species, especially in the eastern United States, produce nuts that are just too tiny to be useful. You don't have to learn all the species of pines to know which ones are edible. Just pick a cone and if the nuts inside are too small, look for a different type of pine. Most of the time large cones contain large nuts, though there are exceptions. The Whitebark pine, a timberline tree in the western United States, has 2½" cones that yield surprisingly large nuts. These nuts are one of the most valuable edible foods available at high altitudes, especially if you're in trouble. But gather them discriminately. They're also one of the few food sources for the birds and mammals in that particular life zone.

With a few exceptions, pine cones ripen on the branch during autumn, then open and drop seeds (nuts) that either germinate or provide meals for forest animals. Occasionally you'll find unopened cones on the ground, but most of the time cones have to be picked off the tree during autumn. To open a cone, scorch it over a fire to burn some of the exterior pitch off and partially roast the nuts. Place the cone on a rock with the tip straight up (not the end that was attached to the tree) and smash it with another rock until the cone splits down the middle and can be torn apart to remove the nuts. If eaten raw, the nuts have a turpentine taste that I find disagreeable. Heating them drives off that taste, leaving a pleasant-tasting crunchy snack. You can heat the nuts by parching them in a dry frying pan over a fire or by baking them on a hot rock in the sun.

All pine and fir trees have edible parts but some evergreens do not. The Pacific Yew *(Taxus brevifolia)* of the West Coast is poisonous. It yields juicy red berries (not cones) that have a

Fig. 13. Pine cones yield one of the most valuable edible foods available at high altitudes.

Fig. 14. Acorns provide palatable nourishment, but they contain bitter tannic acid which should be leached out by boiling or soaking.

greenish-colored seed sticking in the end of the berry. You may have seen this fruit on the similarly poisonous Japanese Yew which is used as an ornamental shrub around buildings.

Even if you can't tell the difference between maple and oak trees, you can probably recognize the acorns on oak trees. The acorns on the Blue Oak of the West Coast and the White Oak of the Northeast can be eaten raw, but most other species produce acorns that contain bitter, astringent tannic acid that's inedible. As tannic acid is water-soluble you can remove it by boiling or soaking the acorns, producing nuts that are both palatable and nutritious. Acorns were a main food source for many California Indians. They usually leached the acorns in cold stream water, a process that takes hours, sometimes a day, to remove the tannic acid. By boiling shelled crushed acorns for about an hour with three changes of water, you will reduce the tannic acid enough to render edible nutmeat.

Berry Good

Blackberries and raspberries (genus *Rubus*) are easily identifiable, but watch out for the stickers. Blueberries (genus *Vaccinium*) and huckleberries (genus *Gaylussacia*) are also easy to recognize.

Corn-on-the-Cattail

Cattails (genus *Typha*) are one of the few plants that supply useful food throughout the year. You can eat any part of this marsh plant that is not too dry or stringy. In spring the pith of the sprouts is tender enough to be eaten raw. Later in spring the sheathed top spike can be boiled and eaten like corn-on-the-cattail. Pollen from the blooming flower spike can be used like flour. The massive tangled root system can be dug up any time of the year and also eaten. Parts of the roots are similar in texture to potatoes; other parts are very fibrous but still starchy enough to provide nutrition.

Fiddleheads

The young curled spring shoots of the bracken fern *(Pteridium aquilinum)* can be eaten raw or boiled in salted water until tender. These easily overlooked shoots can often be spotted by the brown layer of dead fronds that remain from the previous summer.

Fig. 15. (left) Cattails provide useful food throughout the year.

Fig. 16. (right) Fiddleheads are the young curled spring shoots of the bracken fern; they can be eaten raw or boiled.

Dandelions

Everyone's familiar with dandelions *(Taraxacum officinale).* They're abundant in the mountains as well as in your front lawn. Now they're even showing up in salads in health food restaurants. The pale base of the leaves and the greens can be eaten raw, but after the plant blooms the leaves become bitter. The root and greens may be eaten any time of the year after they've been boiled for a few minutes each time in several changes of water to remove the bitter taste.

CRISPY CRITTERS

Some information to follow on edible animals and insects—eat ant larvae, pull wings off grasshoppers so they go down your throat more smoothly—will probably make a lot of people think "Oh yech!" Well, yech is right. But if you were stranded in the mountains with nothing to eat, this juicy information could save your life. A lot of the techniques for catching and killing various animals are brutal and also illegal. The only time they should be used is in a life-threatening situation.

Snakes, Snails, and Tadpole Tails—Plus a Few Other Delicacies

Little animals such as grasshoppers and various other insects are the most abundant and easiest to catch. Grasshoppers have been eaten live in swift gulps by hungry people. (Pulling the wings off won't make them tickle so much going down.) Catch them with your hands if you're quick enough or pin them under a coat or pack. Grasshopper hunting is only worth the effort if a lot are around. You can also eat raw ants and ant larvae, but it hardly seems worth the effort unless there's absolutely nothing else available. Grubs are the white larvae of certain insects; they contain considerably more protein than ant larvae. You can also use them as fish bait. Dig them from moist rotting logs or leaf mulch and loam in damp woods. They're also found in small streams as the stick-and-stone mobile-home building larvae of caddis flies. If you're really starving, eating grubs probably won't be that awful. Some people actually like the taste, but there are ways to make them more attractive to eat. You can cut off their heads, wasting some nutritional value, then boil or broil them. Probably the best thing to do if you're

really squeamish is to close your eyes and swallow real fast
without chewing. That way you'll get some nutrition without
being too grossed out.

Certain species of snails are considered delicacies by some;
however, many of the types found in fresh water are hosts to
various mammalian parasites. They should be avoided as food
or at least thoroughly cooked first.

Frog legs are one of the more epicurean foods found in the
mountains (unlike grubs, at least you see them on restaurant
menus). During the day you can catch frogs by hand in small
streams and shallow pools. The pickerel frog *(Rana palustris)*
of eastern North America has poisonous skin which should be
removed before eating. You can identify this frog by the rows
of square or rectangular spots on its back (instead of the circular spots characteristic of leopard frogs) and bright yellow or
orange coloration on the inside surface of its hind legs. Although I've never eaten tadpole tails, I would imagine they are
also a practical food source.

Since toads are poisonous to eat, they should be distin-
guished from frogs as a survival food. They're terrestrial animals with dry warty skin, unless they've just come out of the
water. Frogs, on the other hand, are aquatic animals with relatively smooth moist skin.

Freshwater clams and mussels which are found in streams
and lakes at lower elevations are safe to eat as long as the water they're in isn't polluted. Select healthy specimens which
will close tight with the slightest disturbance. You can boil or
steam them open. Never eat raw saltwater shellfish. Even healthy ones can be extremely toxic if certain species of plankton
are present in the water. Sometimes even cooking won't de-
stroy the toxin; if you're really starving, cook the shellfish and
eat only a small portion. Then wait a few hours to see if any
poisoning symptoms like numb lips or abdominal cramps appear. If nothing happens, the fish is probably safe to eat.

The eggs from birds, snakes, lizards, and turtles are edible
if cooked, but they're usually well hidden and hard to find.
Turtle meat is delicious; turtles can be easily spotted and
caught in shallow ponds or on land. Lizards, another good
food source, can be caught with thread, grass, or fishline
nooses and sometimes even by hand in cool shady areas where
they tend to be rather sluggish and slow.

Snakes, especially rattlers, are heavy-bodied and provide lots of tender, tasty meat. But they've been completely exterminated in many areas and face extermination in others so only eat them as a last resort. (Also, before you go chasing snakes, read the section on snakebite in Chapter Five.)

Rattlesnakes are rarely found in cold, alpine environments, but I've seen them at 13,000 feet in warm Mexican mountains. In North America during the late spring and fall they can be found sunbathing on the rocks of south-facing slopes. During the summer look for them on flat rock slabs in dry areas not far from water. If it's extremely hot or cold, snakes usually hide under rocks, so watch your fingers if you're doing any rock turning.

Snakes can be killed by smashing them on the head with a club or stone. Even dead, a snake can bite by muscular reflex action, so carefully pin the smashed head and cut if off. And even the severed head can bite so bury it under a stone so no one will accidentally touch it. Snakes can be easily skinned by splitting the belly with a knife and peeling off the skin. If you don't have a knife, start at the neck and pull the skin off inside out, like taking off a sock. The entrails can then be easily scooped out. Boil, broil, or fry the meat either on the bone or filleted. Snake meat is both delicious and nutritious.

FURRY CRITTERS

Porcupines are one of the largest North American animals that can be caught and killed without any special equipment. Sloth-like in disposition, they don't like to move unless heavily pressured. A porcupine walking along the ground is so slow-footed you can easily chase it down. Porkys feed primarily on the inner bark of trees, leaving abundant evidence of their presence on bark-stripped tree trunks; trees they've completely girdled will often have dead tops. To be sure the bare spots you find on tree trunks were made by porcupines, inspect the ground at the base of the tree for their manure, which is sausage-shaped and about 1 to 1½ inches in length. If the droppings are dark brown, moist, and obviously fresh, then a porcupine is probably still in the vicinity. Scan nearby trees carefully, looking for a dark blob with a fuzzy-edged silhouette. After spotting porky in a treetop, you face the problem of getting the animal down. Throwing rocks will just drive porky higher in the tree. The only method I know is one I once used

on a very hungry day. I started climbing the tree porky was
sitting in; it climbed even higher. So I kept climbing. Eventually porky reached the top of the tree. As I got even closer, ax
in hand, the animal released all holds and dropped straight towards me. Fortunately I was practically on the opposite side
of the tree, so it didn't land on my face, but I was impaled by
a couple of quills as porky glanced off my leg on the way down.
The animal hit the ground with a thump and began to run at a
speed slower than me trying to run with a limp. I quickly
climbed down the tree, caught, and killed the animal. I then
had tough, rubbery, filling porcupine stew for dinner.

In the open a rifle or ax would be handy for killing a porcupine but even a club will do. You'll have to hit the animal over
the head which can pose a prickly problem. When threatened
they bristle and point their heavily armed posteriors towards
danger. However, agile feinting to one side or another should
allow you to get a safe crack at porky's head. These animals
can't throw their quills, but they have ten-inch tails that can be
suddenly whipped back and forth, driving quills deep into whatever flesh is smacked. These quills aren't poisonous but they
do have tiny barbs on the ends which work deeper into flexing
muscles, eventually causing infection or even piercing internal
organs. Remove any quills promptly but snip the opposite, exposed ends off first. The barbs in the quills tend to rip flesh
when pulled out; sometimes snipping off the ends makes the
hollow quills collapse and thus easier to remove. Treat the
pierced area like a normal puncture wound.

Getting at porcupines in their dens of hollow trees or rock
caves requires some ingenuity. Since a porcupine will often lie
inside the den entrance blocking the opening with its body,
you can catch porky in this position with a sharp, barbed spear.
Den entrances can be spotted by the pathway of manure in
front—sometimes it's a foot deep with a few quills scattered
around too.

Rabbits are tasty, but the meat is very lean. The famous
Arctic explorer and writer Vilhjalmur Stefansson, in explaining
the importance of fat as well as meat in a carnivorous diet, reported that a diet of jackrabbit meat alone would eventually
lead to what Arctic natives call "rabbit starvation." This
doesn't mean that rabbit meat has no value in a survival situation. Nutritionally rabbit meat provides 490 calories per

pound. As long as you eat it along with other types of survival food, you'll be okay.

Ground squirrels are easier to catch than rabbits. Several methods are effective and all of them are cruel by SPCA standards and probably yours too. But when you're starving and nothing else is available, there's no time to start thinking about how cute the little critter is. All of the squirrel-catching techniques take advantage of the fact that a squirrel chased into its hole will usually come back out within fifteen minutes. The squirrel won't just rush out of the hole, but emerges cautiously, first sticking its nose out about an inch sniffing for danger, then crawling out a few more inches, looking around again, then finally coming out all the way and standing up for a good look around.

After chasing a squirrel into its hole, wait for it to reemerge; then either stab it with a knife or a pointed stick. Stick the knife into the dirt above the burrow about one or two inches back from the opening so the point protrudes into the burrow. Then lie quietly beside the hole with your hand on the hilt of the knife until the squirrel sticks out its nose. A quick thrust with the knife should impale the squirrel.

Another technique involves making a noose of wire, string, nylon fish line, or a shoelace. Arrange the noose around the entrance in a loop large enough for the squirrel to get its head through. Lie down quietly by the burrow about three feet away. When the squirrel comes out and is halfway through the noose, pull the end of the line, drag the squirrel away from the burrow, and kill it with a club.

The third squirrel-catching technique is more reliable than the others but you'll need a three-pronged treble fishhook. A size eight or ten hook is best. Attach a line to the hook and place it at the base of the mound of dirt in front of the burrow entrance with the barbs pointing toward the burrow entrance. The line from the hook should lead around the far side of the burrow entrance over to your hiding place. Wait until the squirrel comes out; then pull on the line and snag the squirrel on the hook. This method can also be used on marmots and woodchucks, but they're more leery than squirrels and sometimes don't come out of their burrows until hours after being chased inside. Also an angry marmot on the end of your line could be dangerous. They have ferocious tempers.

If you're unexpectedly facing a long stay in the wilderness,

Fig. 17. When chased into its hole, a ground squirrel will usually emerge cautiously within fifteen minutes. One trapping technique involves setting a noose around the entrance hole.

consider snaring a deer. One deer alone will provide the bulk of your nutritional requirements for months. Look for a narrow and usually distinct path created by the frequent passage of deer traveling between favorite spots. Also look for fresh deer feces to confirm recent use. The feces are usually loose groupings of oblong pellets about half-an-inch long. An op-

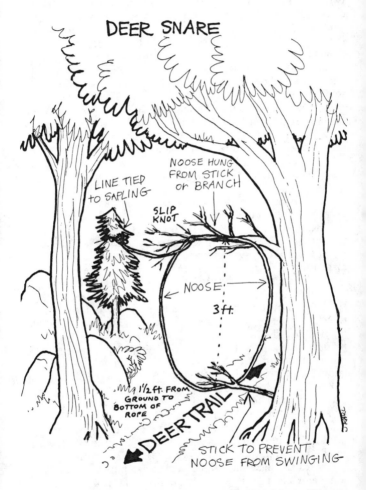

DEER SNARE

LINE TIED
to SAPLING

NOOSE HUNG
FROM STICK
or BRANCH

SLIP
KNOT

NOOSE

3 ft.

1½ ft. FROM
GROUND TO
BOTTOM OF
ROPE

DEERTRAIL

STICK TO PREVENT
NOOSE FROM SWINGING

Fig. 18. An optimum site for a deer snare: if successful, you'll have enough food for an unplanned lengthy stay in the wilderness.

timum site for the snare would be where the trail goes between
two trees a few feet apart. Use light nylon line (parachute
cord) and hang a large (three-foot diameter) noose vertically
between the trees with the bottom of the loop high enough off
the ground for the deer to get its neck, but not its legs, through.
Since deer have a keen sense of sight and smell, rub the noose
in the dirt to change the color of the line and to erase human
odor. Drape the line across a branch sticking partially over the
trail to keep it from swinging in the breeze. Anchor the other
end of the line to a springy branch or sapling so the deer will
be pulled back gently. If the line is anchored to a rigid tree
trunk, the deer could snap the line by lunging suddenly. The
deer probably won't strangle in the trap but will have to be
killed with a club or knife. If this sounds gruesome, remember
we're talking about Stone Age survival, not weekend picnics
in the woods.

In subfreezing weather, skin and quarter the deer right
away, so the skin does not freeze to the flesh. In warmer
weather the skin should be left on the gutted carcass. Hang
the carcass so other animals can't reach it; cover the chest cavity or fill it with leaves and pine needles so flies can't lay
maggot-producing eggs in the meat. A hanging carcass will be
edible for about two days in 70° to 80° weather and up to a
week in 40° to 50° weather. Hunters often hang deer to age
the meat—a process of tenderizing from bacterial decay. While
the meat is aging, you can live off the heart and liver saved during field dressing.

Deer meat can be preserved by turning it into jerky, that is,
dried meat. Slice the meat into strips about a half-inch thick or
less. (The thinner the strips, the quicker they dry.) If you have
salt and pepper on hand, rub them into the strips to speed the
drying process and retard spoilage. Now place the meat strips
on a rack about six feet above a small fire with just enough
heat to dry (not cook) the meat over a ten-hour period. If the
meat isn't completely dry or if it gets cooked instead, it will
spoil. If dried properly, the jerky will last for months.

Snares and deadfalls can be used to catch deer as well as
other animals, and they usually require a minimal amount of
equipment. But unless you're trapped in the backcountry for
more than a few days they aren't that useful. Also in bad

weather animals won't emerge from their dens to be snared. But on the slight chance that you may need to snare an animal, here are a couple of methods that are fairly easy to initiate even if you've never snared anything before.

Setting bait increases the chances of an animal showing up at a certain spot. Use seeds and nuts for squirrels; smelly food like onions, orange peels, bacon fat, or fish entrails for raccoons, opossums, and skunks; and salt or salty leather (gloves, boots) for porcupines and deer. Once you've found a way to lure the animal, you're ready to build the trap.

If you have some light wire (28 gauge), hang some nooses over pathways to snare animals like squirrels and rabbits running in either direction. The noose should be big enough and poised far enough above the pathway so only the animal's head and neck get caught. If their legs are also caught, they might be able to push through the noose and escape. Since animals instinctively run from danger, instead of backing off from the pull of the noose and getting out, they'll charge forward and either strangle themselves or become exhausted struggling to get free.

The figure four deadfall technique is a classic triggering arrangement. A heavy weight like a log or boulder is poised over the baited stick. When the animal begins to eat the bait, the weight falls on the animal. Although simple in concept, the

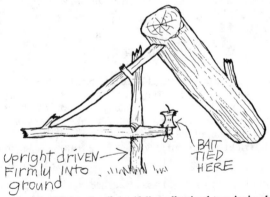

Fig. 19. The "figure four" deadfall small animal trap is simple in concept but can be tedious to build.

figure four is tedious to erect and pretty low on my priority
list of survival projects.

Skinned and Dressed

Small animals like rabbits and squirrels can be skinned and
dressed rapidly by making a short incision at the head or belly
and then pulling off the hide in one or two pieces. Porcupines
don't have quills on their bellies so they can be skinned and
gutted just like other animals. Make an incision on the belly
from breastbone to anus, without puncturing the abdominal
cavity. On large animals extend the incision along the inner
skin of each leg. Gutting an animal involves slicing into the
abdominal cavity (avoid puncturing organs for less mess) and
removing the organs from the esophagus to anus. If internal
organs are injured when you kill an animal, gut it within a few
hours so the meat won't spoil. The heart, liver, and other internal organs on large animals can provide nutritional meat.
Don't eat any organs or flesh that look diseased. Everything
should look just like beef organs in supermarket meat counters
except for lacking the cellophane wrapper. Birds need not be
plucked but can be skinned and gutted even though some nutrition is lost with the skin. Fish don't usually need to be
skinned, but the coarse scales on some species should be
scraped off. If you don't have a knife, improvise by smashing
one rock against another, then breaking the weaker rock into
sharp-edged slivers.

FISH STORIES

Fish are an easy source of food, especially when spawning
or during dry spells when they become trapped in small pools.
If fish are present in streams or lakes, you'll probably see some
as you walk along the bank. Obviously the easiest way to catch
fish is with a baited hook or a dry fly and line. But if you don't
have the right equipment, try one of the following techniques.

Look Ma, No Hands

Catching fish with your hands, called tickling or Indian fishing by poachers, is possible as long as the fish are at least ten
to twenty inches long; it's also much easier for you in small
streams that aren't freezing cold. Locate spots in the stream

where fish are likely to hide: beneath an undercut stream bank, a log, or a large rock. Undisturbed fish usually face upstream in their hiding places so most poachers prefer to start downstream and work towards the fish from behind. They either wade slowly upstream or lie on the stream bank with one arm dangling in the water feeling underneath the bank or a log for a fish. When touched, a large fish usually doesn't become alarmed and swim away. Instead it may actually let you stroke it's belly, which seems to have a mesmerizing effect. You can then move your hand slowly forward and either grab the fish at the gills (don't try to grab the body; it's too slippery) or encircle the head with your thumb and forefinger so it can't swim away. Then with the palm of your hand lift the fish out of the water and flip it onto the bank. This technique takes practice; most people aren't successful the first time so keep trying.

Fig. 20. Tickling fish: instead of darting away, a large fish will often let you stroke its belly, lulling it enough for you to catch it.

If you find yourself chasing a fish that isn't going for the tickling routine, take off your T-shirt and make a fishnet trap. Tie the neck and sleeves closed, then prop the shirt in the water at one end of the pool where the fish has been swimming. Try to chase the fish into the shirt. Ridiculous as this scheme sounds, it actually works quite well, which is probably why it's illegal!

COOKING WITHOUT UTENSILS

You don't really need pots, pans, and grills to cook survival dinners. Pieces of meat or small birds and animals can be speared on a stick (of green or live wood so it won't burn quickly) and broiled over a fire. To fry or steam food, build a fire on top of a flat rock, then sweep the fire off the rock when it's quite hot. Put the food directly on the rock if you want to fry it; surround the food with vegetation like green onions if you want it steamed. The rising liquid vapor of the vegetation will serve to steam your food.

Boiling water without some type of container is practically impossible. Some American Indians carved bowls out of wood or made tightly woven grass baskets that hot rocks were placed in to cook soup, but weekend hikers caught in a sudden storm aren't about to sit around weaving baskets. Either carry something to boil water in or plan on baking, frying, or broiling all your food.

COOKING WITH UTENSILS

Stoves

There are numerous lightweight stoves available. Primus, Optimus, Svea, Phoebus, and MSR are all reputable practical white gas stoves. Prices range from $19 (Svea) to $47 (Optimus 111B). These stoves are economical to operate although carrying and pouring gasoline poses special problems. Don't try to fill a stove inside a tent. If you spill some of the fuel a flash burn could occur when you light the stove. The same thing can happen when you refill a hot stove; cool it off with snow or cold water first.

To avoid the hassle of pouring and priming—preheating by pouring and burning a teaspoonful of fuel over the fuel tank—some campers prefer to use stoves that run on butane fuel in canisters. Bleuet, Gerry, and Primus are reliable brands that range in price from $12 to $20. They're more convenient than gas stoves, but expensive in fuel consumption and they don't operate that well when the canisters are cold.

Carrying gasoline in a pack can be a problem. I'll never forget one winter camping trip in the Adirondack Mountains; a few drops of white gas leaked from my fuel bottles onto my peanut butter and jelly sandwiches. For the next two days I avoided open flames because I intermittently burped hydrocarbon fumes and was afraid I'd blow up! Some plastic bottles will hold gasoline without leaking; to be safe, fill the bottle with gasoline a month before your trip, let it sit outside for a few days, and watch to see if the bottle dissolves. You can also use sturdy, aluminum fuel bottles with metal or tough plastic screw-on caps with 1/8" gaskets.

If using a stove for the first time, cook a few meals in your backyard before a trip. Then you'll know the quirks of that particular stove before you're out in the open. It's also a good idea to relight a stove for a few minutes before subsequent trips to make sure it hasn't been damaged or clogged in storage. An essential accessory with any stove is a thin wire or a special needle to clean the burner tip orifices since they will eventually become clogged from carbon buildup.

Cookpots

My favorite set of cooking pots is the Sigg cooker: two lightweight aluminum pots, a combination frying pan and pot with lid, and a recessed base that holds a small Primus or Svea gasoline stove. Everything fits into a neat little package. Many other practical cookpots are available at backpacking supply stores, each suited to particular needs. If you have a stove with a base and frame you can even use pots and pans from your kitchen. A few wide-mouthed, screw-top plastic containers are valuable for carrying gooey items like peanut butter, margarine, etc.

LIGHT YOUR FIRE

In a true survival situation I wouldn't think twice about building a giant bonfire if it would help save my life. But under normal conditions and especially in areas frequented by campers, a fire really isn't appropriate anymore because of its environmental impact on the forest. In true wilderness areas, firewood is abundant and one person can't do that much damage. But in crowded areas the dead wood is being stripped from trees faster than it can be replaced naturally. The result is a loss in natural cover for wildlife and a disruption of the natural food cycle that starts with the tiny creatures who feed on dead wood. Most experienced backpackers now carry gas stoves which are more convenient than firewood for both cooking and washing. I've spent hundreds of nights in the backcountry without ever building a fire. I either cooked on a gas stove or ate cold food on climbing bivouacs. But there are times when a fire may be the only way to stay warm or to prepare food.

Lighting a Fire Without Matches

Obviously it's easiest to start fires with matches from a waterproof container, but if you don't have any matches there are ways to start fires without them. These methods can and should be learned and practiced at home.

1. A metal match, a commercially-available product, is made from special metals that produce hot sparks when scraped with a knife. If the sparks fall on good tinder like cotton lint or toilet paper (especially if it's sprayed with insect repellent) a flame can be produced.

2. A flame can also be produced by focusing the sun's rays through a magnifying glass or telephoto camera lens onto tinder.

3. You can use fine grade steel wool and flashlight or automobile batteries to start a fire. Stretch and twist the wool into a wire about eight inches long. Place each end of the steel wool on the ends of two batteries, lined up as they would be inside your flashlight. The steel wool will then start to burn and can be placed under tinder.

The flint-and-steel or bow-and-drill methods of fire starting popular in most survival manuals aren't realistic in foul weather survival situations. They're difficult to use under ideal conditions (warm weather, no wind, dry wood), and if you're caught in a rainstorm with your hands and mind numb from the cold, these techniques become practically impossible to apply. So if you don't have the more conventional firestarters like matches or a lighter, you should probably forget about building a fire and concentrate on building a dry, snug, wind-proof shelter.

Six Steps to Firebuilding

A fire is most essential to survival when the weather is cold and wet. Despite miserable conditions, if your matches are dry you should be able to get a fire going even with wet wood.

Follow these six steps.

1. **Collect the firewood.** Don't settle for anything that won't burn well. Even if it takes an hour, gather branches that snap crisply when broken. Green or live wood will bend instead of snap. Rotten wood, which will burn but won't support a fire, will crumble apart rather than snap. Use dead branches from evergreen trees to start the fire as they catch fire and burn quickly even when damp. Use hardwoods from deciduous trees to provide steady, long-lasting coals. Collecting firewood from the ground is less devastating to the forest, but the dead lower branches of standing trees, especially evergreens, are more valuable in a survival situation. They tend to stay drier longer than wood on the ground and they dry more quickly after a storm. Other valuable fuel sources are undecayed hollow tree stumps or the black cores of old pine trees. They're usually full of pitch and burn well even when wet as does bark from white or paper birch trees. Even after days of steady rain it's possible to find dry twigs and kindling materials under overhanging boulders or large logs. If you can't find any dry kindling twigs, try to gather those that have lost their bark—they'll dry more quickly. Or you can split larger twigs lengthwise with a knife and expose the dry inner core. If nighttime is approaching, gather the firewood before you do anything else. It's far easier to build a shelter by firelight than to locate wood in the dark.

2. **Select a site for the fire.** If it's snowing, snow bombs will drop from the outermost parts of the tree branches overhead. Situate the fire either close to the trunk where the bombs won't hit or away from the tree altogether. Ideally the fire should be within arm's reach of your shelter so you can add fuel while sitting comfortably inside. Since mountain storms typically have frequent wind shifts, it doesn't really matter where your shelter is in relation to the fire. Sooner or later smoke will be blown in your face. If it isn't snowing, choose a site in soft dirt or gravel so you can scrape a depression about six inches deep to block the wind while you're lighting the fire. When you leave, refill the depression with dirt and stir well to extinguish the flames. Sift through the dirt with your fingers to make sure the fire is out, then camouflage the site with more dirt, sticks, and rocks to minimize the visual impact. Of course, if you're lost and you think people might be looking for you, don't disguise the fire. Leave it and your shelter as evidence

of your presence. Also leave a note with your name, the date, time, and direction you're heading.

3. **Prepare the firesite.** Build protective windwalls of logs, bark slabs, snow blocks, and rocks if it's windy. Don't use stream rocks for a firewall. They tend to be waterlogged and can explode when steam pressure builds within the rock pores. If it's raining, build a roof four or five feet above the fire with

Fig. 21. To protect a fire until it's burning well enough to keep going in the rain, erect a cover four or five feet above the fire using bark slabs or a poncho.

bark slabs or a poncho to protect the fire until it's burning well enough to keep going in the rain. If the snow's not too deep, dig to ground level for a solid fire base. Often the snow depth under thick evergreens is shallow even when there's ten feet of snow out in the open. If the snow is deep, lay a thick base of wet logs or bark slabs on the ground to keep the fire from melting into the snow and putting itself out. For maximum efficiency build a reflector on the opposite side of the fire to throw more heat into the shelter. Use lightcolored bark, rocks, snow, or a Space Blanket.

4. **Prepare the kindling.** Keep it as dry as possible. If the twigs aren't wet clear through, shave away the damp outer portions with a knife. Sliver the larger twigs with a knife to make thin kindling which will burn more easily. Paper is a good fire starter, but in wet weather it's usually too damp to be of any use. Smearing Vaseline liberally on the twigs will help them burn, as does spraying aerosol cans of insect repellent on them—these contain a flammable hydrocarbon propellant. Stack the kindling in a tepee, lean-to, or criss-cross shape with a space underneath the pile for matches, pitch, or whatever type of starter is being used. Place about two fistfuls of extremely thin (match stick size) twigs on the bottom with thicker twigs above. Stack the pile so it's higher than wide; the heat that rises from the starter will dry the wood above.

5. **Light the fire.** If the wood is wet, you'll need a starter— a short candle stub is good. Place the candle underneath the kindling and light it. For the first ten or fifteen minutes it will look like nothing is happening. But the heat from the candle is actually drying the wood above and eventually the twigs will start to burn. The candle stub technique is a remarkable gimmick and really needs to be seen to be fully appreciated. The idea is so simple and the material so common it's easy to underestimate its value. Although a candle is the most convenient way to ignite wet wood, military surplus heat tabs, Sterno, or barbecue starter bricks can also be used. Throwing gasoline on wet wood to make it burn doesn't work that well. The fire will flare temporarily but not long enough to dry the inside of the wood. Eventually the fire will subside into a pile of smoldering twigs. Cross-country skiers can use their waxing torches to dry the twigs before lighting. If you're without any of the above-

mentioned starters, use pine pitch, the sap that oozes out of scars on pine trees. Pitch is usually available wherever coniferous trees grow. Pine pitch, like candles, needs a wick. If you can't find any pitch-impregnated bark to serve as its own wick, add other wicking materials like dried pine needles or paper match sticks. Since burning pitch can be blown out by the wind more easily than a candle, it needs even more wind protection.

6. **Stack the remaining wood supply,** once the fire has started, beside or even over the fire to dry, then pull it inside your shelter until needed. As you feed the fire remember this Native American adage: "Indian builds small fire, gets up close, keeps warm. White man builds *big* fire, keeps warm running for more firewood." Ordinarily you should build an Indian fire unless the fire is on deep snow. Then a small fire will slowly sink into snow even with a thick bark-slab base. A large "white man's" fire will melt into a wide pit as it sinks. Once the fire reaches the ground the pit will be large enough for you to step into and sit out of the wind with snow walls reflecting the fire's heat onto both the front and back of your body.

Words of Wisdom Learned the Hard Way

During a severe snowstorm in February 1976, another mountain guide and myself were sent out as an advance party to determine if some backpackers were lost on Yosemite's Half Dome. Just before nightfall we reached timberline and were informed by radio that people were definitely trapped on the summit. A full-blown rescue effort got underway and we were told to dig in and wait for the support group. To keep our packs light we hadn't brought a tent, sleeping bags, or stove. But we weren't worried. A couple of veteran outdoorsmen like us shouldn't have any trouble constructing a cozy shelter, right? Well, not exactly. We found a partially sheltered spot next to a boulder and built a framework of branches for the roof and sides, then laid pine boughs over the frame for insulation. We draped our ponchos over the top for a secure snow- and water-resistant shelter. We built a fire in front of one open wall of the shelter and placed a large rotten log on the opposite side of the fire for heat reflection. Congratulating ourselves on the fine job we'd done, we crawled inside to catch a few hours of sleep before the other rescuers arrived. That's when the problems began.

As the blazing fire warmed our shelter, the ice that had frozen around the pine needles of our roof began to melt and drip, creating a miniature indoor rainstorm. My partner decided to crawl out and stand in the snowstorm rather than be drenched by the downpour inside. But I put on my rain parka and stubbornly sat inside, trying to maintain some semblance of dignity as the drops splashed on my clothes and equipment. After about twenty minutes all the ice melted, the dripping stopped, and our shelter was snug again. My partner came back in, and we were just drifting off to sleep when we realized it was a little *too* warm and a little *too* bright inside. We opened our eyes and discovered our roof was on fire. The rotten log we'd used as a reflector had burst into flames that were spreading across to our shelter. We immediately threw snow all over the log to douse the flame, moved it a few feet away, then once again crawled inside our shelter to sleep.

About this time the wind changed direction and our little home became congested with smoke drifting from the fire and the smoldering log. For a while we endured the smoke, coughing and muttering oaths, waiting in vain for the wind direction to change. Finally we got up again and using bark slabs as shovels, moved the fire about fifteen feet away from the shelter so we would be free of drifting smoke. Since the rotten log was full of enough pitch to serve as long-burning fuel, we stuck one end in the fire and went back to bed. Fortunately the next hour passed without incident, so we were able to get some rest before the first support group arrived. They waded out of the knee-deep snow into the glow of our campfire to find us settled comfortably in the shelter. When we got up to greet them, they complimented us on the fine job we'd done preparing camp. Rather than admit the truth about our blunders, we quickly looked away and changed the subject. Our reticence was mistaken for modesty, so our secret remained safe until this confession, made to assure readers that the author speaks from experience—sometimes good, sometimes . . . well, you know how it is.

WE'RE IN THE MOUNTAINS, WHERE'S THE SPARKLETS?

Water is much more important than food in a survival situation. Without water a person can die in a few days; without food a person can last several weeks. Dehydration also increases your susceptibility to fatigue, frostbite, altitude sickness, pulmonary edema, and hypothermia.

In the cold, dry air typical of the mountains, respired water loss alone can exceed two quarts a day. Water requirements vary from about a half-gallon a day for an inactive person to two gallons a day for a person exercising strenuously.* Since you might be unable to find water if you are lost, maintain a good fluid intake even when you're not thirsty. Sip water whenever it's convenient at springs and streams along the trail. Conserve the water you're carrying. Forcing liquids at breakfast and dinner may be appropriate, especially if you're already so exhausted from the day's workout that the idea of melting snow or fetching water seems overwhelming. Remember that rehydration is an important step in relieving fatigue. Reasonably frequent urination and colorless urine are signs of adequate fluid intake.

A deficiency of sodium and potassium salts in the body is commonly associated with dehydration and can be caused by excessive perspiration. These minerals are essential for proper nerve function and muscle contraction. A common symptom of "salt" deficiency is cramping of the arm or leg muscles. Even a large fluid intake may not relieve the cramping symptoms until these minerals are replaced by salts from your diet or the ingestion of salt tablets. A word of caution about salt tablets: if you don't drink enough water with them, you may get sick. Wash down each tablet with at least one cup of fresh water.

Several powdered food products are available to add flavor and nutrition to the water in your canteen. Wyler's and Kool-Aid consist mostly of sugar. Gatorade and ERG contain some beneficial minerals as well as sugar. All of these products seem more satisfying to me diluted to half the concentration suggested on the package, that is, a package that usually makes one quart mixed with two quarts of water. Recent medical research indicates the body can absorb water and salt more easily when concentrations of sugar are diluted.

Streams, Lakes, and Hidden Water Sources

When you're looking for water the most reliable sources are lakes and streams. The solid blue patches or lines on topograph-

*J. A. Syrotuck, *Mountain Medicine Symposium*, p. 30.

ical maps represent lakes and streams that contain water throughout the year, with possible exceptions during prolonged dry spells particularly along the upper reaches of streams. If you encounter a dry stream bed where you expected water, either travel to a larger stream indicated as permanent on the map or wander on down the first stream bed—surface water might not be too many miles away.

If you don't have a map, check canyon bottoms for water; also lush green vegetation indicates a spring. Seepage through the ground and porous rock purifies spring water so unless the water is very slow moving or stagnant, or there is some sign of animal pollution, you can usually assume the water is safe to drink. Springs may be found anywhere: low valley bottoms, hillsides, or high windblown ridges. In some regions, particularly the Appalachians, springs are abundant but so shallow it's often necessary to dredge a depression in the mud and wait for the water to collect and clear.

Even when the streams below mountains are dry, sometimes on high barren slopes there is delicious cool water in tarns. These alpine ponds, usually found above timberline, are fed directly from melting snow so they don't have inlets or outlets. Though this water isn't moving, it rarely requires purification because of its untainted source. Seldom are there enough animals or humans in these areas to contaminate the ponds; the intense sunlight tends to kill any bacteria that happens to form. So drink your fill at high altitude tarns, but remember that any nonmoving water below timberline may be polluted.

Another summertime source of liquid above timberline is patches of snow from the preceding winter, some of which even last through autumn. These patches always produce at least a trickle of water on the slope below, although occasionally it is inaccessible beneath the boulders. In summertime you can also collect the water that drips from icicles in the moat, or gap, between the rock and ice around the edge of a glacier snowfield. At times I have been able to channel four or five drips together by sculpting with my ice ax to form one steady stream flowing into my water bottle. Water from streams immediately below glaciers is often cloudy with glacial silt and should be filtered before drinking.

In areas with heavy annual snowfall, streams are sometimes hidden under the accumulated snow shaded by trees but ex-

posed in the sunny meadows with shallower snowpack. Even
if you find an uncovered stream, it may be out of reach at the
bottom of a narrow crevice formed by banks of snow. Getting
water from the stream without falling in can be a challenge.
One technique for an agile skier or snowshoe expert is to
straddle the stream, one ski on each snowbank, carefully stepping lower and lower into the gap. One misstep means a sudden dunk in the icy stream. On a sunny day this may be just
comical, but in cold weather it can quickly cause hypothermia.
If your legs aren't long enough to straddle the gap, either excavate the snowbank until you can step down to the water level
without any acrobatics or use a canteen tied on the end of a
stick or ski pole to dip water from the stream while you stand
safely on top of the snowbank.

A similar water accessibility problem occurs in the New Eng-
land mountains where snow depth isn't that great, but continuous subfreezing temperatures cause thick ice formations
over creeks. My solution is to carry a three-foot siphon tube
that I lower through a hole in the ice and use like a straw to
suck the water from the stream.

Snow Cones

There's a lot of confusion about the safety of directly eating
snow in a survival situation. During a 1973 Oregon snowstorm,
a woman died after eating snow in an attempt to maintain milk
production to nurse her baby. Yet some mountaineers "eat"
handfuls of snow routinely; they don't suffer ill effects because
they melt the snow in their mouths before swallowing it. Swallowing a chunk of snow would be like swallowing a huge gob
of ice cream—it would hurt your mouth and cause stomach
cramps. So if you have to "eat" snow, melt it in your mouth
first. This may or may not be harmful depending on the situation. I've often eaten snow during subzero midwinter excursions in the Adirondack Mountains, but only while I was moving and warmly dressed. Then I actually enjoyed the cooling
effect. But if I were sitting around shivering through the night
waiting for morning, eating melted snow would only make me
colder.

Don't eat colored snow. Yellow snow is undesirable for obvious reasons. The red (sometimes green or brown) snow near
the surface of permanent summer snowfields in the high country is called watermelon snow because of its odor. The snow

is colored by the algae *Chlamydomonas nivalis* which, if eaten, could cause a violent case of diarrhea. However, the water that trickles from beneath these snowpatches has always been potable from my experiences.

There are a variety of ways to melt snow for drinking water. Take a bottle of water to bed with you so it won't freeze during the night; then use it as a starter in the morning. If you have to melt snow without a starter don't place a pan of snow directly over a hot fire. The aluminum on the bottom of the pan might melt in those tiny areas not in direct contact with snow crystals. Instead, hold the pan of snow a safe distance above the flame until sufficient snow has melted to provide a cooling layer of water on the bottom. When you travel during the day and sip from a water bottle, add bits of snow to your water bottle. The snow will melt from sloshing around and provide you with a few more gulps of water between camps.

Another way to melt snow during the day is to put some on a dark surface which will absorb radiation from the sun. This method works so well that on the lower slopes of Mt. McKinley our party used a black plastic tarp about twelve feet square to melt all our water. We'd lay the tarp over a slight depression in the snow, then sprinkle a thin layer of snow on top of it. As the snow melted on the sun-warmed tarp, the water drops ran together in the bottom of the depression. Even under cloudy skies, this method works as long as the air temperature is above freezing. During mild snowstorms, the tarp method works even better because it absorbs enough radiation to melt the snowflakes as they fall, making it unnecessary to sprinkle snow on the tarp. Melting gallons of water this way every day considerably reduces the necessity of melting snow with a gas stove. You can also melt small amounts of snow inside a clear plastic bag laid on a dark surface like a blue backpack, or you can spread snow on a sun-warmed rock and collect the drips.

Polluted Water

This is a problem even in the mountains, although the cause may be from Mother Nature and friends rather than from people. Below timberline you should question the purity of any stagnant or slow-moving water even if it is clear. Streams can be poisoned by humans, large animals (especially cattle), or by a dead animal lying upstream. Generally, the chances of finding polluted water decrease the higher you travel in the mountains. Solar radiation and aeration tend to kill undesirable bacteria. Thus alpine streams are likely to be good sources of water with their many cascades mixing air and water, flowing over wide rock slabs exposing the water to sunlight.

Purification Techniques

Questionable water should be purified before drinking; otherwise you could wind up with a case of nausea and diarrhea or, more seriously, hepatitis, cholera, typhoid, or (yech!) parasites. Filtering followed by chemical or heat treatment is the most practical way to purify water. Halazone tablets, which contain chlorine, are becoming obsolete mainly because their potency decreases with age or exposure to heat or air; anyway they won't kill the microscopic "bugs" in heavily contaminated cold water. Iodine tablets retain their potency longer than halazone tablets, but they don't work well in cold water. The chlorine in laundry bleach can be used to purify water and so can tincture of iodine. Add a few drops of either purifier to a quart of water and wait about thirty minutes. If the odor of chlorine or iodine isn't detectable from the water, repeat the dosage. A solution of iodine crystals in water can be used in the same way.

If you don't have any chemicals, filter, then boil the water for ten or twenty minutes. I've used this method successfully many times, drinking Amazon River water, cattle-fouled river water in the desert, and the extremely questionable water from the edge of a Peruvian burro pasture. But I sure boiled the hell out of it first!

Chapter Four:
Foul Weather Hazards

I hope you'll never have to deal with frostbite, hypothermia, avalanche, or any other mountain hazard. But it's important to know how to handle these situations, or better yet, how to prevent them from happening in the first place.

HYPOTHERMIA—BETTER KNOWN AS EXPOSURE

One often hears on the news about someone dying from "exposure," a layperson's term for hypothermia. Simply put, hypothermia means the body loses heat faster than it can produce heat. Of all the many mountain hazards, hypothermia is the most serious because it's so sneaky. It can occur just about anywhere; the temperature doesn't even have to be below freezing. Hypothermia can happen at 50°F during a rainstorm, on the beach, or even on a cold night in the desert.

One of my closest brushes with death (and my introduction to hypothermia—I didn't even know then what the word meant) happened on a high north face of Wyoming's Grand Tetons. A sudden snowstorm had trapped my climbing partner and me. Our only refuge was a shallow ice-choked cleft in the rock. By huddling together we managed to shiver miserably through the first night and the next day of near-blizzard conditions. The storm continued into the second night and our prospects for survival grew dimmer and dimmer. We were already worn out from the climb when the storm hit and as it got worse, we became stiffer, colder, hungrier, and wetter—ideal conditions for hypothermia. I'd been shivering for over twenty-four hours as the second night began. Every time I'd fall into a fitful sleep, I'd jerk awake in the throes of violent shivering. I've never shivered so hard for so long. Technically speaking I was experiencing the first stage of hypothermia although I didn't know it then. I did know what freezing to

death meant and grimly realized I was about to become a human popsicle if the storm lasted another day. All I could do
about it was shiver, shiver, shiver.

By dawn on the third day, the sky cleared, the wind dropped,
and the surrounding peaks began to glisten from the sun. My
partner and I stiffly unfolded our bodies from our would-be-
tomb and slowly headed down the mountain. We realized then
that the obvious hazards like rockfall, avalanche, and lightning
were actually far less threatening than the quiet, invisible power of hypothermia.

Hypothermia usually occurs when a person is exposed to
wind, rain, and cold without adequate clothing or shelter. Body
temperature starts to drop causing a series of physical effects
that eventually lead to death.

The time required for hypothermia to progress through each
stage can be a matter of minutes if a person is immersed in ice-
cold water or several days if involved in a situation similar to
the one I described.

If you're caught unexpectedly in a storm, keep an eye out
for the initial signs of hypothermia. Shivering is probably the
best indicator. Fatigue, a few chills, or fumble fingers might
not indicate hypothermia, but if you or someone else is shivering uncontrollably, then the warning alarms should start to go
off because body temperature is beginning to drop. You're not
in serious trouble *yet* but you could be soon if you don't do
something about it immediately. A person in second stage
hypothermia will be unresponsive, detached, uncommunicative,
and unable to think clearly enough to correct the situation.
This last reaction especially will allow rapid deterioration eventually leading to unconsciousness and ultimately death.

Learning to recognize the signs of hypothermia is vital, but
knowing how to prevent it from happening altogether is equally
as important.

Hypothermia Prevention

To a large extent, the ability to withstand hypothermia depends upon one's physical condition before the problem occurs. A rested and well-fed person will have more resistance.
Get a good night's sleep and eat a filling, nutritious breakfast
before going out. Take high energy food with you and snack
often. Don't hike yourself to exhaustion; reserve some energy
for emergencies. Carry foul weather clothing and use it *before*

you get wet. If caught out overnight, hole up in a shelter and conserve your energy. Don't be afraid of freezing to death in your sleep. If you get cold, you'll wake up just like you do at home when the blanket slips off the bed on a chilly night.

When hypothermia is a serious threat, preventive measures will fall into one or the other of these categories: slowing heat loss from the body, or increasing heat production and input into the body. The body loses heat four ways: by radiation, conduction, convection, or evaporation. By understanding exactly how the body loses heat, you can help prevent it from happening.

Radiation

Radiation occurs when a relatively hot material exists in a cooler environment. A hot stove loses heat to a cold room. Similarly, outdoors during a storm, your 98.6° body temperature will radiate heat to the cold air. Clothing tends to insulate your body from this but any bare parts like hands, neck, or head will continue to radiate heat. On a blustery cold day an unprotected head or neck can lose more than half the heat the body is producing.* You can slow radiant heat loss by wearing gloves and a hat—you'll feel twice as warm. A Space Blanket will also help if you're sitting around waiting for a storm to end. It can be folded into a tiny, lightweight package that fits conveniently into a pack, then unfolded into a large thin sheet of aluminized plastic. You can wrap it around you or spread it over several people. The silvery surface of the aluminum reflects most of the lost body heat directly back to the body again, cutting total radiant heat loss tremendously. The flimsiness of a Space Blanket restricts its use to one-shot emergency situations, but it's one of the best survival items you can carry.

On a clear night a black sky will absorb great amounts of heat from the earth and any warm body exposed to it. Rapid cooling by radiation to a black sky is what causes summertime morning frost in mountain meadows. At night the air temperature often drops below freezing. As meadow grass cools because of radiation, frost forms. However, the ground underneath trees will be free from frost because the thick branches form a protective barrier between the ground and the black sky, thereby stopping radiant heat loss. It's actually warmer

*Theodore Lathrop, *Hypothermia, Killer of the Unprepared*, p. 30.

under a tree than out in an open meadow. In a survival situation don't sleep under the stars. Get a roof over your head, whether it's a tent, a lean-to shelter, or just the thick branches of a tree.

Conduction

Heat loss also occurs when your body has direct contact with a colder material that draws heat from you. This happens when you grip a cold steering wheel—your hands become instantly, painfully cold since heat is being drawn from them. Gloves serve to insulate you from such conduction heat loss.

In the backcountry snow is a good insulator, but not in direct contact with your body. Insulate yourself from snow, cold rocks, or frosty ground if you must spend the night outside. Sit or lie on a foam pad, extra clothing, pine needles, bark slabs, shoes, a first-aid kit, rope, skis—anything that's nonmetallic. If your foam pad isn't particularly thick, keep some sweaters or other clothing within reach to slide under the pad if cold spots develop around your shoulders, hips, or feet during the night. The Space Blanket is a reflector, not an insulator—it won't stop conductive heat loss. If you put it on the snow and then lie on it, you'll get cold fast, so put it over you as a reflector.

Convection

Scientifically speaking, convection means movement of a fluid substance. For survival purposes, and simply put, it means wind. Wind chill is a term used to describe the cooling effects of moving air. A person standing in a gentle breeze (10 mph) at a temperature of ten above zero will lose heat just as fast as if the air temperature were a bitter ten degrees below zero with no wind. Reducing convection heat loss is simple: get out of the wind or put on windproof clothes. Normally you can avoid the strong gusts that hit mountain ridges by scrambling a hundred feet or so down the side of the ridge or by taking shelter in the middle of a large, dense cluster of trees. Above timberline you can build a windwall of rocks or snow. A windbreaker, raincoat, or poncho will protect the warm layer of air around your body from being blown away. Our friend the Space Blanket can also be useful as it is impervious to wind.

Fig. 22. (top) The four types of heat loss—evaporation, radiation, convection, and conduction—contribute to the risk of hypothermia. (bottom) Protection of the body against hypothermia is essential to your survival.

Evaporation

Everyone's familiar with heat loss from evaporation of
moisture from wet clothes and skin. Another form of evaporation often overlooked that deserves special explanation is
evaporation of moisture from the lungs. It's a subtle process:
although cold air cannot contain very much moisture, if that
same air is heated it then has the capacity to hold a lot more
moisture. When you inhale, cold dry outside air warms up as
it passes down your throat into your lungs. This warm air absorbs moisture from your lungs. Then your body in turn heats
the liquid water in your lungs, changing it into water vapor.
When you exhale, the air gets cool again and comes out as con-
densation—the fog on your breath. In a hypothermic situation,
you've not only lost water but also the heat that converted the
liquid water in your lungs into vapor. This heat is extremely
important. Consider what happens when you put a lid on a
pot of boiling water on a gas stove. The water will keep boiling with just a small flame, but if you take off the lid and let
the steam rise, you have to turn up the flame to keep the water
boiling. A bigger flame is needed to compensate for the additional heat lost when the boiling water turns into steam and
escapes from the pot. It takes a lot of heat to produce a few
curls of water vapor whether in a pot or in your lungs. If
you're sitting in freezing air, evaporative heat loss may be as
much as fifteen food calories* out of a total metabolic rate of
150 calories an hour. That is, approximately 10 per cent of
the energy you need to stay warm is unusable because it's lost
in the fog, so to speak.

There are two ways to slow evaporative heat loss from the
lungs. One method is to build a small well-insulated draft-free
shelter. Soon after you're in the shelter, the still air around
you will become warmer and more moist from your own body
heat and respiration. Eventually you won't be inhaling cold
dry air with each breath but warmer rehumidified air that
won't absorb water from your lungs. The second method—if
you can't build a shelter—is to place a scarf or some article of
clothing, preferably of wool or synthetics, over your mouth
to breath through. The material will become warm and moist

---

*See "Airway Warming in Accidental Hypothermia," in *Mountain Medi-
cine and Physiology,* for a particularly clear and concise explanation
of moisture/heat loss.

from your breath and will preheat and prehumidify the air
going into your lungs.

I've used the second method often when my sleeping bag
didn't provide enough protection from bitter cold night air.
After pulling the neck extension of my knit cap down over my
mouth and breathing through the cap, I've felt much warmer.
Some people bury their heads inside their sleeping bags to preheat and pre-moisten their inhaled air. But since the sleeping
bag loses some of its insulating ability when moist, it's more
efficient to keep your head out of the bag and cover your
mouth.

Turn the Heat On, Not the Person

The second general method of hypothermia prevention
(mentioned a ways back) involves increasing heat production.
Strenuous exercise produces heat, but eventually you'll get
tired, making you even more vulnerable to hypothermia. Unless you know you can reach a warm house or car within an
hour, vigorous exercise isn't a good idea. If you're facing several nights out in the cold, try to conserve energy. There are
other ways to get warm.

Eating quick-energy foods will keep you warmer. Sugary,
easily digested foods like candy bars, dextrose tablets, and raisins are good choices especially if you start to shiver. Cheese,
meat, and nuts will only make you colder because energy is
needed to digest them. Foods with protein and fat provide
steady, long-lasting energy. They should be eaten at breakfast
and as trail snacks during the day before you get too cold to
digest them. Hot liquids are a good way to warm a shivering
body. Hot tea, hot chocolate, even hot water will help heat internal organs. A stiff shot of brandy might feel great going
down, but it's not good in a hypothermic situation. It will give
a temporary surge of energy, but the prolonged dilation of skin
pores and capillaries will increase heat loss long after the energy
effects have disappeared.

A victim of second-stage hypothermia is too cold to get
warm again simply by crawling into a sleeping bag but needs
additional heat from other sources. If taken to a hospital, the
person would be rewarmed slowly because of the possibility of
death from rewarming shock. However, in the backcountry
the chance of rewarming a hypothermic victim too quickly,
short of throwing him into a hot spring, is minimal. If possible,

get the person indoors in front of a fire or put him in a car and turn the heater on. Remove any wet clothing and get the victim into something dry. Hot drinks are good if the person is conscious. If you're stranded outdoors, have the victim sit in front of a fire with a reflector wall on the opposite side or better yet two fires with two reflectors.

If you can't get a fire going or if it's more practical to rewarm the person in a sleeping bag, be sure to put something warm inside the bag with him. Hot water bottles are excellent assuming you can heat the water. One hot water bottle at the bottom of a sleeping bag has kept my feet and boots pleasantly warm during subzero nights in Alaska. Three or four plastic or metal canteens filled with boiling water (wrap them in cloth to prevent burning) are tremendous heat generators inside a sleeping bag.

Another source of warmth is the body heat from another person who isn't suffering from hypothermia. The victim and the healthy person should huddle together, preferably in a sleeping bag. Both people should strip down to their underwear for maximum skin-to-skin heat transfer. Since this could

The Stages and Physical Effects of Hypothermia

	98.6°F	
FIRST STAGE	• • •	Violent, uncontrollable shivering, fatigue, chills, clumsiness, fumble fingers (blood circulation to extremities is restricted)
	95°F	
SECOND STAGE	• • • •	Numb fingers and toes, rigid muscles, lost coordination, impaired speech, confusion, amnesia, disorientation, uncooperativeness *—shivering may stop*
	90°F	
THIRD STAGE	• •	Unconsciousness, slow respiration, blue skin, weak pulse
	85°F	
	•	Cardiac arrhythmia
	80°F	
DEATH	•	Cardiac arrest
	75°F	

save a life, don't hesitate to jump half-naked into someone's
sleeping bag just because the person isn't your type. However
if the hypothermia victim is your type and you've been dying
for the chance, believe me, now is not the time. Maybe later,
when recovery sets in. After all, this will make you something
of a hero.

FROSTBITE

Frostbite, the freezing of body tissue, can occur when flesh
is exposed to temperatures of $32°F$ or less. With proper treatment even severely frostbitten body parts can be restored without loss of tissue. However, you can do all sorts of things to
prevent frostbite from occurring in the first place.

Fingertips on Prevention

A variety of factors contribute to frostbite. Obviously, im-
proper clothing is one. Smokers won't appreciate one more
piece of negative news, but nicotine causes constriction of the
blood vessels near the skin and reduces resistance to frostbite.
So try not to smoke if frostbite is a concern. Since dehydration
also contributes to frostbite, always drink adequate amounts of
liquids. Touching cold metal on cameras, ski bindings, or bottles rapidly cools skin. In bitter cold conditions metal can actually become bonded to your skin because it freezes the moisture in your flesh, just like when your hands stick to an ice-
cube tray or the handle of a car door on a frosty morning.
Usually blowing on the site will release attached fingers, but
it's best to wear gloves when handling cold metal. Volatile
liquids like gasoline also increase the chance of frostbite if
they spill on your skin.

When standing around in extremely cold weather, vigorously
wiggle toes and fingers to enhance circulation. Numb hands can
usually be warmed by hugging them under your armpits or by
swinging them in circles. If they're still cold, put them inside
your clothes next to the warm skin of your armpits or groin.
Numb toes can be warmed by massaging them or by sitting
next to a fire, but the best method involves planting bare feet
on a friend's bare belly. This method won't work, though, if
clothes remain between feet and belly. Now you can find out
who your real friends are. I've used this method myself quite

successfully. Once while trudging towards Mt. McKinley, one of my partners suddenly realized he couldn't feel his toes. We stopped right there on a barren windswept slope in freezing weather and took off his shoes and socks. I put one of his feet underneath my shirt on my bare stomach. His other foot went up another friend's shirt. About fifteen minutes later his feet were warm and sensitive again. This incident illustrates how you can prevent frostbite despite miserable conditions. Even if you can get back to a warm house or a car within an hour, stop and take care of your feet or hands immediately if they start to feel numb. Then you won't have to treat frostbite back home.

What To Do If Bitten

Since frostbite rarely hurts, sometimes it's hard to know if you've got it. As long as you have feeling in your fingers and toes, they're not frostbitten. Even if they hurt, they're okay. If they're numb, they might not be frostbitten yet but could become so without any warning.

In the case of superficial frostbite (also called frostnip) the skin freezes but the underlying tissue remains unaffected. After it thaws minor blistering might occur, but there's rarely any permanent damage. With severe frostbite, skin, muscles, and sometimes bones freeze. This is serious stuff. Usually the frostbitten area looks pale and feels like wood because the water in the tissue has turned into minute ice crystals. *Don't* rub or massage the area because the ice crystals will slice into the surrounding flesh. Most doctors recommend immersing the frostbitten area (usually hands and feet) into water that's about 110°F until the tissue thaws. Keep replacing water that has cooled with warm water. If you can't measure the temperature of the water, just make sure it's warm but not really hot. Never use direct heat from a fire because frostbitten areas feel so numb a person could actually be burned and not feel it. After the frostbitten parts have thawed they'll look rather gruesome. Huge blisters will form and in the weeks to come the area will turn red, purple, gray, and black. Healing often takes months. However, if treated gently and kept sterile and warm, even black portions will eventually slough away revealing healthy tissue underneath.

Fig. 23. Snow blindness—sunburn of the cornea—is caused by intense solar radiation, especially when amplified by reflections from rocks and snow. Protect your eyes, especially on bright days at high altitudes.

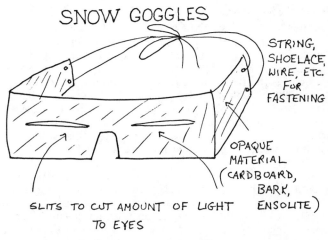

SNOW GOGGLES

STRING, SHOELACE, WIRE, ETC. FOR FASTENING

OPAQUE MATERIAL (CARDBOARD, BARK, ENSOLITE)

SLITS TO CUT AMOUNT OF LIGHT TO EYES

Fig. 24. Improvised goggles can be made from wood, paper, canvas, cardboard, or ensolite.

SNOW BLINDNESS

Snow blindness is essentially a sunburn on the cornea of the eye. It usually happens to people who don't wear sunglasses in areas above timberline where intense solar radiation is amplified by reflections from rocks and snow. People who've experienced snow blindness say it's excruciatingly painful; it feels like grains of sand are in your eyes. What's worse, if travel is necessary, a victim of snow blindness will have to be led by the hand.

Snow blindness symptoms don't always show up until several hours after exposure. The same thing happens when you get a sunburn at the beach and don't discover its intensity until later in the shower. Without a doctor's care little can be done to cure snow blindness immediately. However, it will cure itself in time just like a regular sunburn. Avoiding light and covering your eyes with a cool wet compress will alleviate some of the pain. If you do get to a doctor, your eyes will usually be treated with an antibiotic ophthalmic ointment like Neosporin; you may also be given pain pills.

Put Some Shades On, Man

Snow blindness is a perfect example of the ease and importance of exercising prevention since simply wearing sunglasses or even a hat can protect you. Sunglasses should be a prerequisite on any winter or high altitude trip. Any type of sunglasses is better than none, but in snow country, red- or yellow-tinted glasses or polarized lenses aren't as effective as regular dark glasses. Yellow-black cadmium-coated Vuarnet sunglasses are particularly good for snow travel. Ideally, the design of the sunglasses should minimize the amount of light that enters from the sides, yet allow enough ventilation so the lenses don't fog.

The threat of snow blindness is such that most experienced mountaineers carry an extra pair of sunglasses in case the first one breaks. If you don't have any, make your own from wood, paper, canvas, cardboard, or ensolite. Cut thin slits in the material for your eyes and tie the improvised goggles to your head with string or a cloth strip. You'll look pretty weird walking around with a piece of wood or cardboard on your face, but anything's better than sunburned eyes.

ALTITUDE SICKNESS

Altitude sickness can occur at elevations of 8,000 feet or more. Since the air pressure decreases as you gain altitude, your body has to go through certain physiological changes in order to receive a sufficient supply of oxygen. The process of adjusting to high altitudes is called acclimation or acclimatization. Until your body acclimates to a change in altitude you can experience altitude sickness. The severity depends on one's resistance and the degree of altitude. Usually a person will experience nothing more than headache and nausea; sometimes, though, altitude sickness can be much more serious, even fatal. (More gruesome details later.)

Take It Slow

The best way to avoid altitude sickness is by gaining elevation slowly. How quickly you can ascend without getting sick depends on the overall altitude and the amount of time spent there. Also, individuals acclimate at different rates. If you live at sea level and want to climb a 14,000-foot mountain, ideally you should spend at least three days driving and hiking to an 8,000-foot level. Camp there for several days and take some easy hikes while your body acclimates. Then allow two or three days to backpack to an 11,000-foot level. Spend a couple of days there, then go for the summit. This is the best way for an average hiker who lives in a coastal area to avoid altitude sickness, but it will take about ten days and many people don't have that much time. Consequently they'll try to climb Mt. Whitney in a three-day weekend and get sick. Conservative mountaineers like myself preach against quick climbs, but if you have to do it, I can offer the following advice.

1. Above the 8,000-foot level rapid increases in elevation increase the possibility of *fatal* altitude sickness. Memorize the symptoms of High Altitude Pulmonary Edema and Cerebral Edema and descend at the first sign of these symptoms. Otherwise things will only get worse and pretty soon you won't even be able to walk.

2. Take it easy. Avoid exertion immediately upon arrival at levels of 8,000 feet or more. Heavy exercise predisposes you to altitude sickness, so save your skiing or hiking energy for after your body has adjusted a bit.

3. Get in good shape before the trip. Although this won't directly prevent altitude sickness, you'll have better resistance if you're not suffering from blisters, sore muscles, fatigue, or dehydration.

4. Choose a *reasonable* objective. Instead of trying to do the entire something-or-other crest in one weekend, choose just a portion and enjoy it. Or stay home and bang your head against the wall all weekend. That way you'll get lots of discomfort and still save on gasoline.

5. Allow time for a good dinner on Friday night, a full night's sleep, and a good breakfast Saturday morning. If you do get altitude sickness, those meals and sleep will probably be the last you'll have all weekend.

6. Don't forget to breathe. Seriously. I've been with people who became so detached mentally from the monotony of trudging up a mountain slope they forgot to breathe deeply. As a result their pace became slower and more uncomfortable. I've been able to increase my pace and eliminate altitude headache by hyperventilating—exaggerated inhaling and exhaling. Increase each set of breaths per step as the altitude increases. Near the 20,000-foot summit of Mt. McKinley I was taking ten breaths between each step! That slowed me down a lot, but my pace was steady and eventually I reached the summit without experiencing altitude sickness. Be careful, though; too much hyperventilating at too low an altitude will make you dizzy.

The Symptoms

Medical authorities list three types of altitude sickness: Acute Mountain Sickness, High Altitude Pulmonary Edema (HAPE), and Cerebral Edema (CE). Acute Mountain Sickness isn't that serious and will usually go away in a few days. But HAPE and CE are extremely serious. A person can die from either within as little as twelve hours after the onset of symptoms. Recognizing the early symptoms could save your life or that of a friend.

1. Acute Mountain Sickness usually starts with a headache. As it gets worse the person begins to feel tired, lazy, and slightly nauseous. Some people also experience vomiting and insomnia. Usually these symptoms will go away in a couple of days after you've acclimated or descended.

2. HAPE is similar to pneumonia. The early symptoms are the same as those for Acute Mountain Sickness, plus the victim will also have bubbly breathing, a hacking chest cough that sometimes produces pink frothy spit, gurgling sounds in the chest, and possibly blue-tinged lips due to hypoxia. Eventually the victim will go into a coma and die.

3. CE is the least-common altitude sickness. It involves the accumulation of fluids within the skull causing excessive pressure on the brain. Initial symptoms include headache and difficulty with balance and breathing, followed by delirium, paralysis, coma, and death.

The Cure

The physiological mechanisms that cause altitude sickness aren't completely understood by physicians resulting in some disagreement about proper treatment. Some doctors advocate the use of certain drugs but there's controversy over which of these drugs are best. If you'd like detailed information on the subject, read the *Proceedings of the Yosemite Mountain Medicine Symposium* which summarize the conflict concerning the use of drugs to treat altitude sickness.

For those like myself who aren't medical professionals with a knowledge of drugs, the treatment for altitude sickness is straightforward: GO DOWN! Often a drop in altitude of 3,000 feet is enough to cure the problem without treatment. Oxygen also works, but how many backpackers want to lug around oxygen cylinders? Descending to a lower altitude might alleviate the problem but this won't be easy if the victim is semiconscious and has to be carried or lowered down through rugged terrain. That's why it's so important to recognize the early signs so you can go down before things get worse. Don't sit around waiting for a helicopter or rescue team to show up. They might be delayed and in the meantime the victim could die.

AVALANCHE

The first step in avalanche safety is to recognize and avoid dangerous slopes. Take certain precautions if you *have* to cross an avalanche-prone slope, but it's always safer to choose a dif-

ferent route if possible. These guidelines will help you identify hazardous areas:

1. Always inspect any steep treeless slope or gully where
snow or rockslides can easily occur. Avalanches can happen on
forested hillsides but are less likely since trees help anchor the
snow. Trees are also evidence that the slope hasn't had major
avalanches before, whereas a treeless gash in a forest may indicate an area that frequently avalanches. Slope angles of twenty to sixty degrees are the most common sites for slides. Under the right conditions *any* slope can avalanche so try to tune
your senses to the local snow conditions.

2. Avalanche danger is especially high during and right after storms. A slope that was safe when you started out on a
ski tour might not be safe on the way back during a snowstorm. Snowfall rates of more than one inch an hour cause
very high hazards. This should be foremost in the minds of
powder snow hounds who delight in skiing deep untracked
snow during or immediately after a big storm. Don't let en-
thusiasm overcome good judgment.

3. Avalanches tend to occur in the same places each year,
and the evidence of their paths—treeless vertical strips—is
pretty obvious. Downslanting bushes and trees with chipped
bark and broken branches on the uphill sides of a mountain or
slope also indicate avalanche activity.

4. If an avalanche is actually occurring on a nearby mountainside, don't go onto slopes similar to the one that's sliding.
Sometimes you can spot an avalanche before it happens by
the formation of sunballs—small snowballs that spontaneously
start to roll down a slope, getting bigger and bigger. Or as you
walk you'll hear a hollow sound under the crust of snow, a
sudden whump that radiates away from you or running snow
cracks as you break through the crust. All this indicates tension in the snow and possible imminent fracture.

5. Valuable information about local avalanche conditions
can be obtained from Forest Service or National Park Service
offices. Also for more understanding of snow characteristics
and avalanche safety, read the booklets by La Chapelle and
the U.S. Forest Service or the excellent essay in *Wilderness
Skiing*. (See Bibliography.)

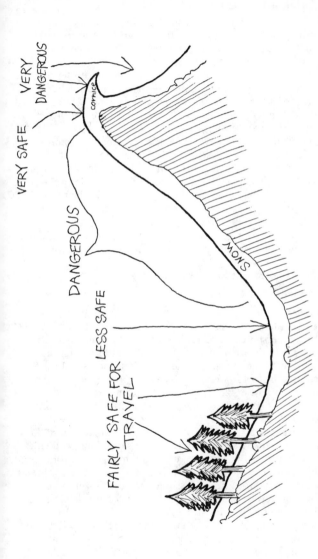

Fig. 25. Learn to recognize and avoid avalanche-prone slopes, choosing alternative routes of travel whenever possible.

The High Road or the Low Road

The existence of an avalanche slope doesn't make safe travel impossible, but you might have to alter your route to avoid one. Before leaving on a backcountry trip make a detailed study of your proposed route on a topographical map. Look for alternatives in areas where the map crosses steep terrain. Broad valley bottoms are usually safer than narrow valleys. The crest of a broad ridge has no avalanche danger, but it might be exposed to wind during a storm and be an ideal spot for hypothermia or frostbite.

If you have to pass across a dangerous slope, try to cross above it on flat terrain near the ridge top. If that's not practical, then cross in the forest beneath the hazardous area. The chance of an avalanche occurring while you pass along the slope is small because most victims trigger their own avalanche. If you're with a group, travel one at a time through the danger area while the others watch from either side and are available for rescue if anything happens. Just because others have skied a slope only minutes before doesn't mean it's safe. In one documented case, a soldier following the tracks of thirty-two of his comrades was caught in an avalanche.

Radio Transmitters and Ropes

Some skiers carry battery-powered, pocket radio transceivers that have proven remarkably effective in avalanche rescue. Each person carries a radio switched to transmit; then if someone is buried in an avalanche the survivors switch their radios to receive and use them as direction-finders to locate the victim. Unfortunately the expense of these radios—the cheapest is about $60—prohibits widespread use.

In hazardous terrain, you can also use an avalanche cord, a lightweight red line about 50 feet long. The cord is tied to your waist and trails behind you while you ski. If you're buried in an avalanche and if you're lucky, part of the cord will remain on top of the snow so rescuers can see it and follow the cord to you. The only objection I have to avalanche cords and radios is that a lot of people assume they can travel in extremely dangerous terrain just because they have these devices. I feel that no one outside of a rescue team should be skiing areas where a radio or a rope might even be needed. If ski conditions seem dangerous, perhaps the day should be spent in a mountain meadow studying Nature or possibly each other.

What To Do If the Roof Caves In

If caught in an avalanche that doesn't bury you, try to call out to others to warn them. Discard ski poles, rucksack, and skis. Make vigorous swimming motions to keep on top of the snow and try to work your way to the side of the avalanche path. If you're buried under snow, try to form an air space in front of your face with your arms before the snow sets up. If possible, dig yourself out, but don't panic and struggle against unyielding snow. Conserve your energy and have faith in your ultimate rescue.

If you see someone disappear under the snow from an avalanche, note the last-seen point in your head, then mark it when the avalanche stops. Survival depends on how fast you can get to the avalanche victim, so this is very critical. Statistics indicate that a person buried in an avalanche has a 50 per cent chance of surviving if rescued within an hour. If a lot of people are available, someone should go for help while the others search.

First make a hasty search downslope from the last-seen point; look for clues on the surface. Use a ski pole or stick to probe the obvious areas like the debris at the bottom and the areas around trees and rocks. If you still can't find the person, systematically probe the entire area below the last-seen point. Probe as deep as possible with spacing about two or three feet apart. Continue probing until there is obviously no hope of quick discovery. Then go get help if you're the only one looking. Although slight, there's still a chance of survival even after burial of 24 hours.

LIGHTNING

The view you'll have if camped overnight on a summit may be exhilarating, spiritual, and great for photographs but it could also be suicidal if a thunderstorm develops during the night. If you're hiking towards a summit on a warm summer afternoon, those white fluffy clouds you see could change within half an hour into dense towering thunderheads. So be prepared to make a rapid descent at the first sign of a nearby storm. However, if the skies are clear overhead and the storm is more than four miles away, don't abandon your plans as many thunderstorms will stay in one area. But keep an eye on the storm and if it looks like it's moving closer, seek safety.

You can estimate the distance of a thunderstorm by counting the seconds between a flash of lightning and the following
thunderclap. The speed of light is so great that a lightning
flash is seen almost instantaneously while the slower speed of
sound requires about five seconds to travel a mile. So if you
hear thunder twenty seconds after seeing the flash, the lightning is about four miles away. If later on the interval between
sight and sound is only fifteen seconds, assume that the storm
is approaching and take appropriate precautions.

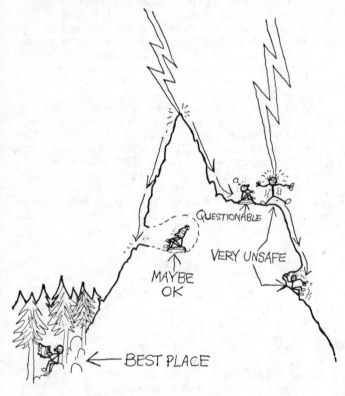

Fig. 26. Sitting out lightning storms: choose a spot that's not a
likely path for lightning.

Sitting Out the Storm

Obviously the safest place to sit out a storm is inside a building; a second and usually more available choice in the mountains is a car. If lightning hits a car, the electricity gets caged around the outside metal framework instead of zapping the people inside. Of course, convertibles and fiberglass-bodied cars don't give this protection.

If a car isn't available, try to choose a spot that's not a likely path for lightning. Generally, the lower the elevation, the better. Always stay away from large bodies of water. A lone tree on a ridge or meadow might be dangerous, but a forest full of trees on the low side of a mountain or valley is very safe.

Sitting out a storm in an exposed area is risky, but if you have no other choice you can do a few things to improve the situation. You'll need to protect yourself from a direct strike as well as electrical ground currents. Try to settle in a low spot or a depression; avoid ridges and lakes. Don't take shelter near a tree that's already been struck by lightning. It will have a split or barkless streak in a slight spiral along the trunk. Keep your body low but don't sit or lie on the ground and expose yourself to ground currents. If possible, sit on nonconducting material like ropes, packs, or ensolite pads, or just squat and hope that the small amount of insulation provided by boots will suffice. Keep all metal equipment such as pack frames and cameras away from you. They won't attract a direct strike, but they will conduct the ground currents that follow.

If you take shelter in a cave, make sure it's deeper than it is tall. Then the ground currents will arc across the mouth of the cave instead of flowing along the roof and back out along the floor. To insure safety inside a cave or beneath a boulder, insulate yourself from the walls, roof, and floor; otherwise you could become a human spark plug for a current shortcut between the roof and floor. The edge of a mountain lake is a great place for a campsite, but if a lightning discharge takes place in the water, tremendous ground currents might be generated along the shore. As of yet, there's no exact figures for what distance from the edge of a lake is safe, but I've lived through some wild Rocky Mountain thunderstorms by lying on foam pads inside a tent about two hundred yards from a lake.

Twice in the Wyoming Rockies I struggled up one side of a mountain only to be met by thunderheads approaching from the other side. The static electricity phenomena experienced under these circumstances are terrifying. There is a sort of invisible pressure in the atmosphere. One time a continuous buzzing noise encircled my head. Another time the rope between my partner and me began to hum like a high tension wire, while the snow around us crackled. Things can get even more bizarre. Others have described such effects as hair standing on end and sparks flying off metal equipment. All of these special effects mean that an electric voltage difference exists between the earth and sky and that a lightning strike is probably just around the next spark. Needless to say you shouldn't stick around for the light show.

Chapter Five:
Other Hazards

Now that I have you thoroughly paranoid about hypothermia, frostbite, and several other disasters, let me lay just a few more on you. Seriously, none of the following hazards have to happen as long as you know what to watch for.

SNAKEBITE

The sudden whirring of a snake in the bushes sends chills down the spine of even the boldest outdoor adventurer. Reactions vary from fascination to blind hysteria. Most of the fear and hostility towards snakes is unwarranted. I was raised in a section of Pennsylvania heavily populated with rattlers and copperheads and worked, much to my dismay, as a rattlesnake bounty hunter at one time (not the greatest of jobs). So I've been in direct contact with hundreds of poisonous serpents. My fellow snake hunters and I agree that rattlers are defensive rather than aggressive when confronted by humans. They'd rather flee than fight. The scare stories I've heard about rattlers chasing humans have probably been told by people who were so terrified they didn't understand exactly what was going on. Once I was chased by a rattler which was actually just heading towards safety, not towards me. Since I was a few yards down the hill from some people who were trying to capture the recalcitrant serpent, it took off in the direction it could travel fastest—right towards me. I was familiar enough with snakes to know that it wasn't attacking me; since we were in the midst of a snake den I decided to just stand there rather than jump aside and possibly land on another snake. As I expected, the fleeing snake sped between my legs and continued downhill without a glance in my direction. If I'd panicked and run down the hill, the frightened snake would have been right

behind me, and I might have had my own spine-tingling chase
story to tell.

Snake Country

With a few exceptions, mostly in the South, North American rattlesnakes aren't found at altitudes over 9,000 feet. If
unfamiliar with an area, ask local residents if the area is populated with poisonous snakes. You can camp and travel safely
in snake-infested country by following these precautions:

1. Stay on roads and trails where you can see the ground.
Wear high boots and long pants for protection. If you see a
rattlesnake on the path, give it a respectfully wide berth and
continue hiking. Stay on the lookout for others. They don't
travel in pairs, but if you've already seen one, others are bound
to be nearby.

2. Before stepping on logs or rocks, inspect the other side
with a stick. If you're traveling through heavy brush, beat it
ahead of you with a stick so a snake can warn you of its presence by rattling. Or push the bushes aside with a stick and
check each spot before walking on it. Always inspect the
ledges of rocks before putting your hands on them. Don't put
hands or feet near any crevices a snake could hide in. Try to
walk on top of boulders rather than alongside them unless
there's danger of falling.

3. Make camp in smooth open areas like wide unbroken
rock slabs, large areas of sand, or patches of short grass that
don't have snake hiding places. It's extremely unlikely that
a snake will enter your camp at night. However, sleeping in a
hammock or inside a fully-enclosed tent will insure safety. If
you sleep in the open, use a poncho or a large piece of plastic
as a ground cloth. Snakes, ticks, chiggers, and scorpions don't
like to crawl on smooth plastic because it offers them little
traction and no protection from predators.

If the Viper Strikes

Despite precautions, approximately 6,000 snakebites occur
every year in the United States, according to the American
National Red Cross, but less than fifteen are fatal. More people
die from bee stings than snakebites.* The symptoms of poisoning by a pit viper are immediate pain similar to a bee sting,
rapid swelling at the site of the bite, and possible numbness

---

*G. Tom Shires, M.D., *Care of the Trauma Patient*, p. 252.

Figs. 27 & 28. Rattlesnakes are defensive rather than aggressive when confronted by humans. They'd rather flee than fight.

spreading from the bite; continued swelling follows, then discoloration and a gradual lapse into shock, faintness, possible vomiting, and cold sweats. Normally, complete recovery follows in one to six days depending upon the amount of venom injected.

Perhaps because of the high recovery rate, medical authorities haven't been able to agree upon the best treatment for snakebite, so it would be presumptuous for me to say one method is better than the others. Instead I'll discuss the pros and cons of the four most popular methods and let you decide which method might be best.

Regardless of which technique you prefer, always try to remain calm if you're treating a snakebite victim. Help reduce the shock the person will be experiencing. Reel off a few statistics on how good the odds are, tell the bee sting story, etc. Also, keep the victim still since the main objective in treatment is to stop the flow of poison through the body.

Before treatment make sure the bite is actually poisonous. It's not unusual for poisonous snakes to bite without injecting any venom into the wound. This occurs approximately one out of five times, according to the *Journal of the American Medical Association.* This could happen if the snake recently emptied its venom sacs into some other hapless creature or if something's wrong with its injecting mechanism. If poison has been injected, the bite will feel like a bee sting and begin to swell. If only dull pain is felt, similar to that from a tetanus shot, the victim should be treated for a puncture wound or animal bite, not a viper bite.

1. **The Cut and Suck Method** is the best-known technique, but it's rapidly losing favor among medical professionals. Red Cross and Emergency Medical Technician manuals still include this method but recommend it only with reservations. The critics are concerned primarily with the danger of increased infection or severed tendons and nerves from the incision and suggest that a negligible amount of poison can be removed. Briefly this technique involves placing a constriction band (not a tourniquet) between the bite and the victim's heart to slow the lymphatic and venous blood return without completely shutting off circulation, then making short shallow incisions over the fang marks and applying suction to draw the poison from the wound. (Don't use your mouth directly on the wound to suck—it's full of germs. Snakebite kits contain suction cups.)

2. **The Ligature-Cryotherapy Method or Cold Treatment** is also controversial. It involves temporarily applying a tight narrow ligature between the bite and the victim's heart, then cooling the bitten area with an ice pack or cold water bath. The victim should then be transported to a medical facility where controlled cooling and gradual rewarming can take place. The disadvantage with this method is that some people develop frostbite because their tissues are cooled too much. And in some situations there might be no way to cool the victim.

3. **The Natural Cure** involves doing nothing except treating the victim for shock. A less widely publicized method, it is still quite successful. The victim should lie down, rest, and concentrate on taking deep breaths to slow the heart beat. Keep the victim covered; offer fluids as desired until the effects of the poison have been overcome. Sweating it out is a good way to describe this method. The Natural Cure is a good alternative to the Cut and Suck Method especially out in the backcountry. It also works best on a large person who has been bitten by a small snake. Another method should probably be used if the person is small, especially a child, and the snake large.

4. **The Antivenin Method** is the most often advocated form of treatment. Antivenin serum consists of antibodies extracted from the blood of horses inoculated with rattlesnake venom. When injected into a snakebite victim, the antibodies are very effective in speeding recovery. One major disadvantage is that approximately 20 to 40 per cent of the population is allergic to horse serum and may become sicker from it than from the snakebite. Another drawback is in remote backcountry antivenin might not be available. Some backpackers carry antivenin kits and a serum-sensitivity needle when they pack far into snake country.

SUMMER SNOW SLOPES

Summer snow slopes, not to be confused with glaciers, consist of coarse-grained "corn" snow. These steep snow patches are encountered from midsummer through autumn in deep gullies or on north-facing mountainsides. They're often safe refreshing places for backpackers on hot summer days and make easier paths for mountain climbers than the surrounding rocks. Avalanches are unlikely on summer slopes especially if they contain the algae-caused red or watermelon snow. However, rockfalls, slippery ice, and hollow spots on summer snow-slopes are just as dangerous as an avalanche. Every high country traveler should learn how to recognize these hazards.

Stoned

Most rockfall danger comes directly from the cliffs above the snow patches. The process of melting and refreezing from summer to winter gradually pries stones and boulders loose. They can come whizzing down a snowslope with such speed even small ones cause serious injury. Gullies are especially dangerous because rockfalls from above are refunnelled into them. The warmest part of the afternoon is the period of most frequent rockfall. A less frequent but equally hazardous event is the sudden release of a "sleeper" boulder—a rock lying on the surface of a snowslope, held marginally in place by friction. The slightest bit of movement can send it barreling down the slope. One time I stopped my survival students at the side of a snowpatch to explain some of the hazards involved. I stepped onto the snowslope and as if on cue, a huge boulder, jarred loose by my steps, came bulldozing down towards me. I leaped back towards my students and watched the boulder hurtle across my tracks and crash explosively below. During the rest of the class the students were wonderfully attentive to my lecture about mountain hazards.

Slip Sliding Away

Snow from the preceding winter commonly melts at the bottom of snowpatches before the top, exposing the ice beneath. As a result the bottom edge of some snowpatches can become dangerously icy while the top section is still mushy snow. A perfect example of what can happen on slippery summer slopes occurred once when my partner and I were following a moderately steep snow-filled gully down towards camp. I started cautiously down the snowslope using a sort of skiing without skis technique known as glissading. The snow was dense but soft enough on the surface for me to dig my heels in and stop sliding if I had to. As I got closer to the bottom I noticed that the snowpatch ended at a short cliff with about a ten-foot drop into vicious-looking rocks. About the same time I also noticed that the snow had changed into slick ice. There was no way I could dig my heels into the ice and stop sliding so I lay down and dug my ice ax in to stop. Then I carefully made my way over to the side of the snowpatch and into the boulders. I warned my friend about the ice and waited at the bottom for him to come down. Unfortunately he wasn't able to dig his ice ax into the slippery ice and continued to slide, going faster and faster as he approached the edge of the cliff. At first I thought I'd try to catch him as he slid over the edge, but as he gained speed it became obvious that I couldn't stop him. Just as he flew off the edge I ducked. He bounced off my back smashing me to the ground, then crashed violently into the boulders. We were lucky. He only sprained his ankle and I got a headache from his ice ax hitting the helmet on my head. But others, not so lucky, have been killed on summer snowslopes.

Hollow Spots

Another insidious characteristic of many snowfields is the presence of hollow sections under the surface usually caused by stream channels flowing beneath the snow. A hiker who falls into one of these hollow spots could become too numb to move after a few seconds in icy water and die from hypothermia within minutes. This clearly emphasizes the importance of avoiding a snowpatch with a stream running underneath it. Hidden channels should be suspected whenever a stream disappears at the upper part of a snowfield only to reappear at the bottom of the field. Sometimes hidden hollows are found near sun-warmed rocks sticking out of a snowfield. These hollows aren't nearly as threatening as water channels, but if you're glissading down a slope and land in one you could break your leg. Move very cautiously on snow that has rocks protruding from it.

Getting Down In One Piece

Obviously it would be safer to stay off icy snowslopes, but if you have to travel down a snow-filled gully or across a steep snowfield during an emergency without special equipment, the following guidelines should help.

1. Try to find a sharp, hard tool to dig into the ice with—a metal drinking cup, a stick, or even a sharp rock will do.

2. Sometimes a small moat or gap exists between the snow and the rock walls surrounding it and can be partially used to

avoid a steep or icy section. Deep moats should be avoided because of the obvious danger of falling into them.

3. If the snow is soft, one of the safest ways to go down a slope is to face it and climb backwards kicking secure footholds into the snow. This is time-consuming but effective.

4. If the slope isn't too steep and you're tired and don't mind a cold rear end, sit on the slope, dig your heels and a stick into the snow, and scoot down.

5. To stop a sliding fall, roll over facing the snow and dig your fingers, toes, elbows, or whatever tool is available into the snow while raising your stomach off the snow to increase pressure on the drag points. This "self-arrest" procedure is especially effective when done with an ice ax.

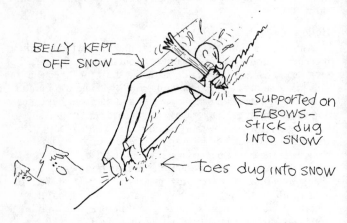

Fig. 29. Use this self-arrest procedure to stop a sliding fall on icy snowslopes.

STREAM CROSSINGS

If you have to cross a stream, rocks often provide a natural bridge. But be careful; sometimes they're very slippery. Small rocks can roll out from under your feet and large ones might not be flat enough to step on or too far apart. Sometimes by searching one or two hundred yards up or down the stream you can find a safe bridge of rocks or fallen logs.

Fig. 30. Often by searching up or down a stream you can find a
safe bridge of rocks or fallen logs.

Wading

If you have to wade across a stream, the shallowest part is
usually where the stream is widest unless the bottom is chan-
neled. The narrower sections are usually swifter and deeper.
Choose a section to cross that is fairly wide and uncluttered by
boulders and logs that might trip or snag you. If the water isn't
too deep or swift and footing is secure, it might be best to
cross barefoot. However, if the water is ice-cold your feet
could become too numb to feel the bottom. Some streams are
swift enough to roll boulders across bare toes, so wear boots if
this is the case. They'll keep your feet warm and uninjured
and improve your grip on the stream floor. Since hiking in wet
socks tends to cause blisters, take your socks off and wade
across with bare feet inside your boots. When you reach the
other side, pour the water out and put your socks and boots
back on. If the boots are waterproofed, they won't soak up
that much moisture in a brief stream crossing. The water level
in snow-fed streams varies depending on the time of day. If a
stream looks too deep to cross, make camp and cross early the
next morning when the water level will be down.

In a serious stream crossing a pole can be used to keep your
balance and probe for deep spots in murky water. You can
usually find a stick along the bank of a stream to use as a pole.
Whether to place the stick upstream or downstream is a moot
point. I prefer the stability of forming a tripod by placing the

stick upstream, facing upstream, legs spread. This places my
torso broadside to the current; I use this method in shallower
streams, as once the water reaches my hips I could be washed
away. Other people recommend facing across the stream with
the pole downstream. This advantageously places the side of
your body towards the current, but balance is more difficult.
The ultimate decision is up to you.

If you're with a group of people, it's easier for everyone to
cross in a line rather than individually. The largest person
should be upstream, the smallest downstream. Face either upstream hanging on to each other's waists, or face across-stream
linking elbows to stabilize the formation. The larger people upstream will break the force of the water before it hits the
smaller people downstream. The people downstream also help
stabilize the larger people. If the water's murky, don't look at
it while crossing because it may confuse your sense of balance.
Instead look at the opposite bank for a stable horizon to orient
yourself.

The Danger of Safety Ropes

Safety ropes can actually be more hazardous than helpful
during river crossings. Once after swallowing several pints of
the Susquehanna River during an attempt to retrieve a sunken
canoe, I realized that the rope connecting me to shore was actually pulling me underneath the water! Another tragic example of what can happen with ropes occurred when a rock
climber actually died at the end of a so-called river safety rope.
He was trying to cross a stream that was close to a waterfall.
To avoid being washed over the falls if the current became ex-
cessively strong, his partner anchored one end of a safety line
to a tree. The current did wash him downstream and the line
held him, but it also dragged him under to the point of drown-
ing. Obviously my faith in safety ropes is nil.

Crossing With Backpacks

When crossing a stream with a backpack, unbuckle the waist
strap in case you have to get it off in a hurry. Keep the pack
on unless it's dragging you underneath the water as sometimes
a pack can help keep you afloat. Twice I've been swept away
in rivers and both times my pack floated rather than sank
which helped keep me on the surface until I regained my
footing.

QUICKSAND

Ever since I watched my first Jungle Jim movie, I've been fascinated by the silent, lethal, bottomless, sucking pools of quicksand that inexorably engulf any man (usually the bad guy) or beast unfortunate enough to wander into them. As a kid I investigated all neighborhood reports of "quicksand" from isolated spots in the country to nearby construction sites. But all I ever found was thick, gooey mud which at worst tended to suck the boots off my feet as I walked through it. As an adult I have backpacked down streams in Western deserts, through bogs in the mountains, across sandbarred rivers in Alaska and the Yukon, even through a couple of Southern swamps. Although occasionally I've been slowed or momentarily stuck in deep mud, I've never seen the type of quicksand so vividly portrayed in the movies. Even so, stories about quicksand continue to circulate. Cattle reputedly have succumbed to quicksand along river bottoms in Utah. In 1975, a California fisherman, mired in quicksand along a tidal flat and threatened by an incoming tide, was rescued dramatically by helicopter. Maybe these incidents really did involve Jungle Jim quicksand, but I suspect that it was just plain old mud combined with a heavy dose of panic on the victim's part. Jungle Jim quicksand probably doesn't exist, especially in the mountains. What does exist is deep gooey sand or mud that any fairly aggressive person could walk, swim, or roll out of.

Knee-deep In Mud

Even though I don't think of mud as a hazard, a person raised with the myth of killer quicksand might panic if stuck knee-deep in river mud. If this happens, vigorous efforts to lift one leg will only drive the other leg deeper into the muck. A calm person could slowly, very slowly, lift one leg out without pushing the other leg in deeper, take a step in the right direction, then very slowly lift the other leg and by repeating this process eventually walk right through the goo. A thrashing person would get nowhere except deeper into the mud. Once while stalking water creatures in a North Carolina backwater, I became embedded hip-deep in mud (quicksand?) but got myself out by using the slow, steady process just described. On the other hand sometimes you can actually walk across the top of fairly solid mud flats you'd sink into if standing still.

Because mud is so full of particulate matter (its buoyancy is about twice that of fresh water) you can actually float on it. A heavy steel bulldozer might sink from sight in deep mud but not a person. If you're in mud that's too deep to get your legs out of, lean sideways until you can lie down and let your legs float out naturally. Then barrel-roll over to solid ground, get up, wipe the mud off your face, and thumb your nose at Jungle Jim!

Chapter Six:
Innocence Lost: Bears

The commotion that occurs when bears saunter through national park campgrounds on nightly raids rivals the hysteria a UFO invasion would create. Frantic campers fly out of tents, hopping around in sleeping bags, banging on pots, yelling, screaming, and taking flash pictures for the folks back home. These episodes are usually nothing more than slapstick comedies with sleep and groceries the only casualties. The next morning the rangers hear all about it for the eighty-fifth time that summer. "He was huge, gigantic, big and black, took an entire package of cookies, even ate the paper . . .!"

Occasionally these raids result in the loss of all food, damaged equipment, and sometimes, though rarely, death. Such misfortune can happen to backpackers in remote areas or to RV enthusiasts parked bumper-to-bumper. There is no foolproof way to avoid encounters with bears; however, the information in this chapter should enable anyone to live in relative peace alongside these furry beasts. In general, peaceful camping with bears depends upon knowing what species of bear is running his paws through your carob bars as some bears are more ferocious than others, making an accurate evaluation of how familiar the bear is with people, and resolving to outwit the bear no matter what elaborate device you might have to use.

THE DIFFERENCE BETWEEN
GRIZZLIES AND BLACK BEARS

Even though zoologists list almost 20 varieties of North American bruins, the only bears most campers are likely to run into are grizzlies and black bears. If you see any polar bears, call the zoo.* Since grizzlies tend to be more ferocious and

---

*Since polar bears are rarely encountered by backpackers, they're not discussed here. However, if you do run into one, treat it like a grizzly.

less predictable than black bears, it's important to know the difference between the two.

Grizzlies (along with their cousins the Kodiak Bear and Alaskan Brown Bear) have distinct humps between their shoulders and short thick snouts. Their fur may be black, brown, or yellowish-brown with a gray wash. If you're lucky enough to catch a glimpse of one from a distance, these beautiful and powerful creatures are an impressive sight. But don't get any closer. Grizzlies have been responsible for some serious injuries

Fig. 31. Snout size and hump appearance are the two major features for differentiating between the black bear and the grizzly bear. Fur color, size, and habitat are the other factors to consider.

and may often try to kill (or even eat) a person perceived as a threat. Their presence justifies special understanding and caution. Most grizzlies are found in western Canada and Alaska, with a few in the Rocky Mountain regions of Montana, Wyoming, Idaho, and northeastern Washington. You can reasonably assume that any bruin you see elsewhere is a black bear— the species most commonly encountered in North America.

Black bears exist not only in grizzly country but also in nearly all forest regions throughout the continent. Unlike grizzlies, black bears have comparatively long snouts and no hump. But they aren't always black. Some are cinnamon or brown; some have a patch of white fur on their throat. Black bears are generally smaller than grizzlies and not as temperamental. When frightened or angered by humans, they'll usually limit their attack to a single swat or bite that might cause serious injury but rarely death. Most of the time all a black bear wants is to get you out of his way, not into his mouth.

BEARS AND FOOD—
GUESS WHO'S COMING TO DINNER?

Bears are not ferocious beasts that prowl the forest growling and licking their bloodthirsty chops in search of fresh tender human flesh. They much prefer candy to people. In fact, some of them will go to the most devious and ridiculous means to get their bear claws on your groceries.

In remote wilderness areas or where hunters abound, bears are very shy of the human scent and will usually avoid your campsite and your food. However, in more popular camping areas, like national parks which are game preserves, bears have lost their fear of the human scent and associate us with only one thing—lots of rich, sugary, plentiful *food*. Look at it from the bear's point of view. When the smell of Oreos drifts through the forest under a bear's twitching snout, the berries Mother Nature intended him to eat seem bland by comparison. Since these bears are "people-wise" (they've been observing us for years), they know they can usually snatch food out from under a camper's quivering, frightened gaze with ease and little hassle.

This condition has led to the nonchalant nightly (sometimes daily) bear raids that create so much havoc at crowded campgrounds. If bears could be weaned from the humans–groceries syndrome, they would return to their natural wild food sources and quit disturbing campers for their source of nutrition. Most bear attacks occur because the animal smells food in a camp-site and starts to prowl the area looking for dinner. Campers hear the bear, then wake up and either frighten the animal into a defensive attack or anger it because the bear thinks someone is claiming food that is rightfully his.

BEAR LOGIC–WHAT'S YOURS IS NOW MINE

Once a bear gets his paws on your food or backpack, it's then his property, not yours. That's how a bear thinks and any attempt on your part to persuade him otherwise will result in trouble. This is an important premise to re-member. A bear circling your camp at dinnertime can be easily chased away, but if he manages to sneak in later and drag a backpack full of food off into the bushes, that pack then be-longs to him. If you try to chase him away from the pack he may stand his ground and possibly attack. Under such circum-stances it's safer just to accept the loss and try to salvage the remnants after the bear has finished ransacking your pack.

A similar possession condition exists when a campground bear raids a garbage can or plunders a bag of pilfered groceries. Although a roly-poly bruin tossing corn flakes into the air may be comical and great material for photographs, don't get too close. The bear might think you're trying to take *his* groceries and charge with surprising swiftness, knocking an eager photog-rapher head over heels into the hospital.

PROTECTING YOUR BODY AND POSSESSIONS FROM LIP-SMACKING, BURPING BEARS

Car-clouting Bruins

People-wise bears in national parks have learned how to break into unattended cars by bending the top part of the door, tearing out a partially opened window, going through the top of a convertible, or simply by smashing a closed win-dow. It's even rumored that they've learned how to get into airtight cars like VW bugs by jumping on the roof to compress it and pop the doors open! If you have to leave your car overnight, special precautions should be taken even if you don't have any food in it. Since these bears have learned to recognize food containers like tin cans and ice chests, they'll go after these items when they see them in cars. So all food containers should either be covered with a blanket and put on the floor of the car or kept out of sight in the trunk. Leave the seats and dashboard of the car uncluttered so the bear doesn't mistake another object for a food container. Food with a strong smell, like fresh fruit or pastries, should be stored in the trunk in an airtight container. If the aroma of the food is too much for the bear, he won't think twice about trying to reach the inside of the trunk by tearing out the back seat!

If you own a convertible, never leave food in it. A bear will go right through your $600 top. Don't even leave sweet-smelling non-food items like suntan oil or hand lotion in your car. A bear won't know until it's too late that Coppertone isn't edible. Car-clouting bruins often return the following night to the scene of their original break-in even if they didn't find any food the first time. So if your window was smashed and the upholstery clawed by a bear, either move the car somewhere else, out of the bear's territory, or be prepared for a second break-in. This time he might enter through a different window and continue to tear the seats apart.

There is some evidence that the odor of mothballs or harsh-smelling cleansers like Ajax or Comet (not lemon-scented types) discourages bears from raiding vacant cars as long as food is properly stored. People who have used mothballs to protect cars left for one or more nights at parking lots notorious for bashing bears have reported complete success. This may be too small a sample of the car-camping population to be significant statistically, but these results encourage further experimentation. Besides, what have you got to lose?

A liberal dosage of mothballs seems to work best. Put about six in the trunk and twelve in the interior of the car. I used this method once along with a sprinkling of Comet cleanser along the outside windowsill of my car which was parked in an area frequented by some particularly adept and ruthless bears. Every night some car in that lot was damaged by bears. Mine went unharmed even with food stored in the trunk, but not

untouched judging from the muddy pawprints on the wind-
shield. The idea behind the cleanser is that the bear will sniff
it into his nose and be discouraged from inspecting the car any
further. That my car remained unscathed during this risky period could be attributed to plain blind luck rather than the
moth ball–cleanser method, but it's worth a try. Chemical protection also seems to protect vacant tents, but more on that
later.

Who's That Sleeping In My Tent?

People-wise bears lured by the smell of food won't think
twice about wandering into a tent, plopping down on a sleeping bag, and gulping the Mars bars stashed under a pillow. Unless you enjoy cuddling up to 300 pounds of fur, it's critically
important to maintain a sleeping area free from food and food
aromas, especially in grizzly country.

Try not to eat in your tent; always remove all food, crumbs,
candy bars, and non-food but aromatic items like toothpaste,
lip balm, skin lotion, and water bottles that retain the odor of
sweet powdered drink mixes. The following true story reads
like something out of the *National Enquirer,* but it proves the
importance of this. A young female camper who had spread a
thick layer of coconut lotion on her face for protection from
the sun woke up during a midday nap in a forest clearing to
discover a bear licking oil off her face with his big, wet, slob-
bering tongue. Despite her fright, she managed to remain perfectly still until the furry intruder had licked all traces of oil
from her face, belched rudely, and departed. She was fortu-
nate. Others aren't so lucky. A young male camper, sleeping
in pants he'd wiped greasy hands on while cooking, was severely mauled by a bear that smelled the grease on his clothes.
Never wipe your hands on your clothes after cooking. Use a
cloth or paper towel that can be burned or tossed into a garbage can away from your sleeping area. Try to leave perfume
and deodorant at home when camping since the smell may
attract bears. (If you're self-conscious, stay downwind of your
friends.) Try to cook dinner at least a couple of hundred feet
away from your sleeping area, and be sure to dump dirty dishwater away from camp.

Even if an unattended tent doesn't contain food, it's still
vulnerable to roving campground bears. Mothballs can help
here. One time I placed about six in the tent and set some out-

side around the edges when I was away from camp on an overnight climb. Nothing happened to the tent and I was in an area
frequented by bears. So it must have worked.

A more "organic" method of chemical protection advocated
by some is urinating on the ground near the tent. The theory
behind this is that a bear will be repelled by the ammonia-like
odor. I experimented with this one summer in an area frequented by a people-wise mother black bear and her cubs. Despite the fact that I took a leak just about everywhere, nightly
tent-pawing rituals occurred regularly for weeks. One night
after returning to camp, I discovered a tear in one wall of the
tent where mama had apparently slashed the material and
poked her head in to confirm that there wasn't any food available. Though slightly disgruntled, I continued urinating around
the tent. But a week later when the tent was vacant one night,
it received two more slashes. When I came back after another
night out the following week, the tent had so many gashes I
could watch the sun rise and set from the inside! Thus endeth
my patience with the "organic" technique of tent protection.

Bears and Backpacks

Even an empty backpack can retain the scent of food, so
store it away from your sleeping area. Not only bears but
little creatures like mice, chipmunks, and ground squirrels are
wise to the edible treasures that are often found in backpacks.
Some animals, especially people-wise bears, will investigate any
neglected pack whether it smells like food or not. Even if the
pack is tied, buttoned, and zipped up tight, these animals will
gnaw or tear holes in the pack until they either get something
to eat or are satisfied that there isn't any food inside. Some
coyotes will even haul a pack off to a hidden place for a more
leisurely inspection. Veteran campers have learned that whenever a pack must be left overnight or unattended even for a
few minutes, all pockets and inner chambers should be left
open. Then the bears and little animals can poke around inside
and see that there isn't any food without ripping or chewing
the pack to shreds.

HANGING FOOD

If you're camping in an area far from civilization—by American standards that usually means away from grocery stores

and gas stations—your survival and comfort are relatively dependent upon keeping food away from marauding bears. Many backpacking trips have been ruined because some lip-smacking bears devoured an entire supply of food.

In remote wilderness areas where bears are more naive about human groceries, simple methods of food storage will probably protect your food. However, in more popular backpacking locales, these bears have become amazingly cunning and brash in

Fig. 32. People-wise bears have become amazingly bold and cunning in their abilities to score food from campers. Working together, a mama bear and her cubs go to great lengths to seize an unwary camper's food.

their attempts to capture food. The sophisticated techniques they employ deserve Ph.D. status in "De-suspension Engineering."

Although people have tried everything from burying food in pits to erecting semi-portable electric fences, the only method that seems to work really well is hanging food on a line from a tree or cliff so the bears can't reach it. (Remember when I said you might have to resort to elaborate means?)

In order to do this you'll need about 50 or 100 feet of a light nylon line and a rock or pocketknife for a weight. Find a long isolated tree limb that's at least twenty feet above the ground. Make sure it isn't close to any objects the bear can climb on. Tie a heavy rock or pocketknife onto one end of the line and throw the weight (with the line following) over the limb. If your pitching arm is weak, then sling the weight over the limb David and Goliath style. If the line isn't released at the right moment, the weight will sail askew and tangle in another tree. You might have to try this a few times. After you have the line over the limb, hoist the food bag (usually your pack or sleeping bag stuffsack) on the end of the line, five feet below the limb, eight feet away from the trunk, and about fifteen feet above the ground. Otherwise mama bear might send her cubs up the tree to grab the bag or out on the limb where their weight will lower it just enough for her to reach it.

Anchoring the opposite end of the line is as critical as the position of the food bag. This was pointedly demonstrated to me one summer evening while I was camping in a semi-remote but regularly used area. As I sat spooning Tuna Noodle Surprise into my mouth, I watched a black bear strolling down through the forest towards me. As soon as the bear saw me, he started to make a detour around my site. As he passed the lines I'd left dangling from a tree to hang the food that night, this amazing creature did a double take, stopped dead in his bear tracks, stared at the lines, and then started to chew them! At that point I chased the bear away and sat down to reflect upon the psychological principles of Pavlovian response and response reinforcement as related to this incident. Apparently experienced bears have learned that sometimes when they bite or break a line a bag of food will fall from the sky as if it were manna from heaven! That's why it is so important to make sure the food line is out of reach and preferably out of sight.

Perhaps the most successful anchoring technique is to weight

ROCK

FOOD BAG

5'

8'

15'

Fig. 33. This hanging technique is the best method for keeping your food from bears.

the line (with a rock or another food bag) so the counterweight hangs alongside the food bag and both objects are well out of reach of the bears. You'll need a stick at least fifteen feet long to push the weight up high enough when you're suspending the bag and also to help retrieve it. The only way a bear can get the food now is if he climbs out on the limb and bites the line so the food drops to the ground. Although I've never heard of any bears who can do this, these shaggy forest acrobats will probably learn how eventually. Then a new suspension scheme will have to be worked out.

If you can't find an adequate limb, string the line from one tree to another, like a clothesline, but high enough so the bears can't reach it. Since there are two places where a bear can bite the rope with this method, it's wise to add a second or even third independent suspension line between different trees.

In certain parts of Alaska, northern Canada, and the northern Pacific coast it may be impossible to hang food because of the lack of tall trees. Since grizzlies inhabit these areas, you should never sleep with food nearby, even to protect it from other animals. The only choice you have in this situation is to store food away from the sleeping area and just hope that a grizzly doesn't discover your cache. If you are in a true wilderness area, you probably won't have to worry since bears in these areas are usually suspicious of the human scent and will avoid your campsite. Of course if the food is just too aromatic and the bear momentarily overcomes his fear of humans, he might start to do a little investigating.

By covering food stores with heavy rocks on the Alaskan tundra and by caching food in the thick branches of small spruce trees in the Yukon bush, I've successfully protected hundreds of pounds of rations from coyotes, wolves, ravens, even grizzlies (who hadn't yet heard about the humans–groceries connection). The only food I've ever lost was some cereal to an unseen rodent.

By now you're probably thinking that these bears are so devious and so determined that no matter how well you protect your food one of them is bound to get it. Well, the real key to saving food from bears is to camp where no one else ever goes. This became very clear to me after a two-day rock climb in Yosemite's rugged Tenaya Canyon. My partner and I walked about 100 feet away from the cliff top into the forest to spend the night. We were too exhausted to hang up our food so we just left everything scattered on the ground and crawled into our sleeping bags. Two short miles away in Little Yosemite Valley the bears were creating their usual nightly havoc–plundering packs, tearing down food lines. Since no one had ever camped where we were, our sleep went undisturbed. When we woke up, everything was right where we left it.

NEVER SAY BOO TO A BEAR

Even if you follow all the food storage and bear avoidance techniques I have mentioned, you'll probably run into a bear sooner or later if you're in the mountains often enough. With intelligence and a clear understanding of bear behavior you can usually handle confrontations with little hassle. Most casualties are caused by ignorance of or disrespect for the bear.

There are certain occasions when a bear should be handled like a time bomb—very delicately. Bears can become extremely dangerous and aggressive in the following situations: a mother bear protecting her cubs, a frightened or threatened bear protecting itself, or a grizzly protecting its territory.

1. A mother black bear is reasonably tolerant of a stranger in the vicinity of her cubs as long as you don't get any closer to them than she is. If a raiding family of black bears has descended upon your campsite in search of a midnight snack, go ahead and chase mom away but leave her kids alone.

Grizzly mothers are even more protective of their young than black bears. They have to watch out for humans *and* male grizzlies who often try to kill unguarded cubs. Since a grizzly mother leads such a nerve-racking life protecting her children, it pays to be extremely cautious when you're near a grizzly family. Maintain at least several hundred yards between you and the bear family in a campground and many times that distance in the backcountry. If you're traveling through sections of thick forest or heavy bush, make lots of noise so the mother will know you're approaching and can either lead her cubs out of your way or at least not be startled and angered by your sudden approach. Even though occasional yodeling, singing, or whistling may disturb one's tranquil communion with Nature, that's quite all right since Nature might otherwise appear in the form of a mad mama grizzly.

2. If startled or cornered, a bear might attack savagely in self-defense. So before you chase *any* bear away from camp or your pack, be sure that the animal has an exit route and won't feel trapped; otherwise he might run right over you instead of around you. If you're walking around at night, especially in grizzly country, carry a flashlight. Bears can't see any better in the dark than humans. Don't walk too quietly, lest you suddenly and painfully collide with an equally startled bruin. Scuff

your feet, clear your throat, or whistle softly so a roving bear can hear your approach and step out of your way.

3. Grizzlies have been accused of unprovoked attacks on humans. In reality, these attacks were probably justified from the bear's point of view. Perhaps a cub was nearby to protect or the bear was frightened by an intruder who had stumbled into its domain. There isn't a lot you can do to protect yourself from accidental run-ins with grizzlies. Just stay alert for their presence and be prepared for a charge.

BAD NEWS BEARS

Once I saw a family run from a picnic table, abandoning an entire meal to a black bear who had appeared on the scene smacking his lips and rubbing his paws in anticipation of all those goodies. Such concessions are entirely unnecessary and only serve to reinforce the bear's impression that humans can be equated with easy food pickings.

Unwanted Visitors

Black bears circling a campsite can usually be discouraged from coming any closer by yelling, banging pots together, or blowing whistles. All this commotion, though, will wake up other campers if it's late at night. A quieter method is stone throwing. *(Never* try this on a grizzly.) Don't try to hit the bear with the stones, just throw them near him. Molesting animals is prohibited in national parks so stoning a bear might be frowned upon. Besides a bear that is being clobbered by rocks might become irritated instead of intimidated, thereby provoking an encounter, not an exit.

Always try to assess the bear's personality and temperament before you do anything. If a bear starts to growl while you're winding up to pitch a rock, then it would probably be smart to find a less antagonistic method. Remember there's strength in numbers, so stay in a group if you can, and never get so close to the bear that he feels cornered.

If you wake up and hear a bear sniffing and pawing your tent, you can usually get rid of him by merely talking so he'll know you're in there. However, if he can smell food in the tent, talking might not work and he could tear his way in. If you're sleeping out in the open and wake up to find a bear

breathing in your face, don't yell or thrash suddenly, startling
the bruin and prompting a defensive attack. Instead, lie still
and subtly let the bear know you're not a rock by breathing
loudly. Then he'll realize you're alive without being frightened.

Right of Way On the Trail—You or the Bear?

If you meet a grizzly or a black bear on the trail, don't drop
your pack and run. People can't outrun bears, despite the popular misconception that because of their short hind legs bears
run slowly downhill. I've watched bears race down hills with
amazing swiftness.

If you've encountered a grizzly on the trail, back away
slowly towards a tree, perhaps talking very calmly to the animal. Keep retreating until you're well out of the grizzly's way.
If you're nose-to-snout with a black bear, just relax and try to
sense how the bear wants to handle it. When I've run into
black bears, they've either retreated or stood there while I
walked around them, naturally at a reasonable distance. Sometimes I've stood there while the bear walked around me, at an
equally reasonable distance.

Sometimes a black bear will be more intrigued by the food
in your pack than with continuing his stroll. If that happens,
you might have to become more aggressive and chase the bear
away, not an easy task. It takes a lot of nerve to get rid of a
bear that's staring you right in the eye. Unless you're Davy
Crockett, grinning won't work. Try yelling, stamping your feet,
throwing stones, or blowing a whistle.

If a Bear Starts to Charge

The safest response depends tremendously on whether you
face a grizzly or a black bear. If a grizzly is charging in defense
of cubs, food, or territory, the animal will probably try to kill
you. If a black bear is charging, he usually only wants to get
you out of the vicinity. So if it's a black bear, RUN. Get away
as fast as you can. Even though you can't outrun the speedy
bruin, once the animal sees that you're rapidly leaving and are
no longer a threat, he will probably brush you off as a nuisance.

I have seen this rapid retreat technique demonstrated dozens of times. A classic example occurred when a national park
employee was dumping his office trash can into an outdoor
container; up popped an angry trash-covered bear. The trash
can went flying in one direction while the startled employee

sprinted away in the opposite direction with the bear in hot pursuit. After a few bounds the bear stopped his chase, secure in the knowledge that the person was a respectable distance away. The bear then waddled back to his dumpster grumbling all the while.

Because it's so hard to predict a grizzly's behavior a lot of controversy surrounds what to do when one charges. Just one whiff of a human and a grizzly may flee or he may decide to put up a fight and defend his territory. Some grizzlies have continued charging despite the noise of rifle shots, while other grizzlies have been beaten off by a weapon as insignificant as a fishing pole. If a grizzly is merely threatening rather than charging, don't run away. Instant flight might trigger an attack. Instead, back away slowly toward a tree or some other protection. If the bear charges, then run to a tree and try to climb it (adult grizzlies can't climb trees). By dropping a hat, coat, or pack on your way to the tree, you might distract the bear and have more time to get to safety. If you're close to a car or building, get inside as fast as you can. Although grizzlies have enough muscle to smash their way into a house or car, they won't usually go this far.

If, God forbid, the beast actually gets his paws on your hide, park rangers suggest that you play dead by lying motionless either face down or curled in a ball with one hand protecting your neck and the other covering your genitals. Hopefully, if you can remain still through some rough investigative pawing and nipping, nothing too serious will happen. The thought of a gigantic grizzly pawing and mauling your body is horrifying. Think about it, though, when you're too tired to dump that dirty dishwater away from camp. Grizzly attacks are sensational when they occur, but are actually very unlikely, especially if you follow the procedures mentioned in this chapter.

SPECIAL WORDS OF WARNING
FROM GRIZZLY COUNTRY

Two special precautions should be considered in grizzly country.

1. Don't pitch your tent close to a riverbank trail because it might be the same path used by a grizzly during his nightly

hunting excursions. Even though some of the best places to camp are along these trails, a grizzly may become violently irate at such a rude intrusion into his territory.

2. There is much speculation that some fatal grizzly attacks have been prompted by female menstrual odors. The evidence isn't conclusive, but it's persuasive enough for me to conclude that if I were a woman, I'd make every effort to schedule my trip into grizzly country when I wasn't having my period.

ONE LAST BIT OF ADVICE

When in bear country, always remember you're in their backyard, not yours. Humans are intruders. Bears have learned a lot about us and this hasn't helped prevent conflicts. Maybe if we learned more about them fewer accidents would occur. By understanding rather than exterminating bears and their environment, people can coexist peacefully with these fascinating creatures. The burden is upon us to learn to live with Nature, rather than to pit ourselves against it.

Chapter Seven:
Getting From Here to There With a Map and Compass

To many people a topographical map looks like an unfathomable mass of squiggly lines that bear little resemblance to the trail you may have just lost. A compass is similarly categorized as a mysterious gadget best left to veteran mountaineers who have managed to unfathom its dark secrets. To these skeptics I dedicate this chapter. There are some valuable methods of navigation that can be easily understood. Follow me. . . .

NATURE'S WAY, WITHOUT A COMPASS

There are several ways to determine direction without a compass. Granted these methods aren't 100 per cent accurate, but in mountain navigation you usually don't need an exact compass reading as much as a rough indication of north, south, east, or west.

Look At the Slopes

A fairly easy way to determine direction involves recognizing the differences between the vegetation and moisture patterns on north- and south-facing slopes. In the Northern Hemisphere, north-facing slopes characteristically receive less sun than south-facing slopes. As a result, they're cooler and damper. In the summer you can recognize north-facing slopes because they retain patches of snow long after it's melted from south-facing slopes. In the winter you can spot south-facing slopes because the trees and open areas will be the first to lose snow and the snowpack will be shallower. Even though this method only gives a rough indication of direction, it can be used when the sun is hidden by an overcast sky—a time when you're more apt to become lost.

The temperature and moisture differences on slopes exemplifies the concept of *microclimate*—a local weather pattern within a larger climate. Often the climate in areas only a mile apart will be drastically different. This is especially evident in valleys that run east/west. On a sunny midwinter's day you can walk around comfortably in shirt sleeves on the north side of the valley, while on the shadier south side, people are wearing parkas and gloves. Making use of these climatic variations can be important in a survival situation. If you're caught in a cold storm, take shelter on a south-facing slope where the ground temperature will be several degrees warmer than on a north-facing slope. In late summer after a hot dusty hike, you'll be more comfortable on the cooler, moister north-facing slope.

Wear Your Watch

You've probably heard about the wristwatch-and-sun method, a popular direction-finding technique. Point the hour hand of the watch towards the sun, then mentally bisect the angle between the hour hand and noon. That direction will be south. This method is based on the fact that the sun rises in the east, sets in the west, and is due south at noon. The only drawback with this particular technique is that the sun has to be out. If it's hidden by clouds, look at the slopes.

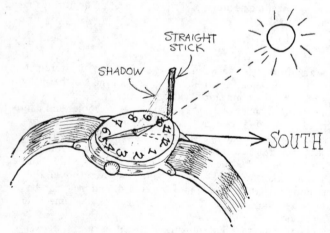

Fig. 34. The wristwatch-and-sun method is a convenient direction-finding technique.

Follow the Streams

Most of the time, following streams and rivers downstream will eventually lead you back to home and hearth, but not always. Some streams in the Brooks Range of Alaska flow away from civilization into the Arctic Ocean. Some streams in the Sierra Nevadas in California will lead you into some very rough terrain—abrupt waterfalls, high cliffs, steep gorges. Use this method only if staying is more dangerous than leaving and you have no other course to follow.

The Moss Method

In North America moss tends to grow on the north side of trees; however, in areas where a damp wind is blowing from the south, guess what? The moss grows on the south side of the tree. In areas I'm familiar with, about 60 per cent of the trees will have moss on the north side; the other 40 per cent will have it on the east, west, or south sides. So use the moss method only as a last resort and with skepticism.

Star Bright, Star Light—Where Am I Tonight?

If you have to find direction at night, turn to the stars. The Big Dipper, Orion, and the Southern Cross are three easily iden-

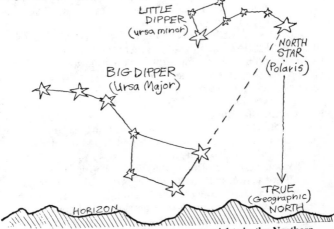

Fig. 35. For finding direction on summer nights in the Northern Hemisphere, use the Big Dipper constellation to locate the North Star.

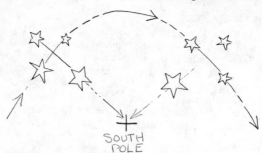

SOUTH
POLE

Fig. 36. The Southern Cross is the Southern Hemisphere's counterpart to the Big Dipper for finding direction: when you face the Southern Cross, you're looking south.

tifiable constellations that have been guiding people for thousands of years. Chances are you already know what they look like, but just in case. . . .

The Big Dipper is easy to spot in the Northern Hemisphere during the summer, but it's rather obscure in the winter. The two stars that define the lip and side of the Dipper point in almost a straight line towards the North Star which is within two degrees of true north. The North Star represents the end of the handle on the Little Dipper.

One time I actually used the Big Dipper in an *urban* survival situation. I'd flown to Houston at night, rented a car at the terminal, and in classic country bumpkin style got lost in a maze of freeway interchanges when I left the airport. I knew I was on the right freeway, but I didn't know if I was going in the right direction. I pulled over, got out of the car, and by locating the Big Dipper determined that I was going the wrong way. (You never can tell when you might be able to use all this great information.) I turned around and continued uneventfully but smugly on my way.

The Southern Cross, a counterpart to the Big Dipper, can be seen in the Southern Hemisphere. Although there is no South Star corresponding to the North Star, the long axis of the Southern Cross points to the part of sky where a South Star would be if it existed. So if you face the Southern Cross you're looking south.

If you're camping in the Northern Hemisphere during winter you can spot Orion. This constellation resembles a hunter with

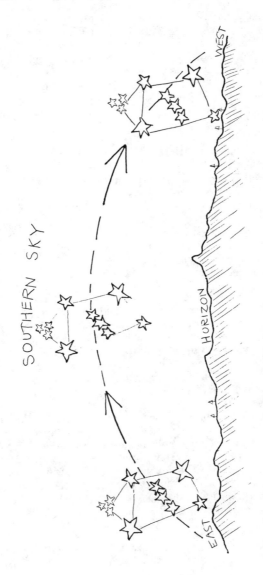

Fig. 37. On winter nights in the Northern Hemisphere, the constellation Orion is visible. The uppermost star in Orion's belt rises due east and sets due west.

a club in one hand, a lion's mane in the other, and a small dagger dangling from his belt. The three stars of Orion's belt and the four stars that define his hands and feet are in the southern part of the sky. If a distant horizon is visible, the uppermost star in Orion's belt rises due east and sets due west as seen from either hemisphere. Once Orion is visible above the horizon the entire constellation is either southeast or southwest, but essentially south.

THE EASIER WAY—WITH A COMPASS

Operating a compass is fairly simple, yet most explanations I've read leave the impression that complex mathematical equations must be followed to work it. That's not really the case. Although a compass can do much more than tell where north, south, east, and west are, most mountain travelers only use it for that. If you already know how to operate a compass and want to get into its more sophisticated uses, wait. That information is coming later.

How a Compass Works

A compass is merely a magnet in a box. You could make one yourself with a simple bar magnet suspended from a string tied around the middle of the magnet. Once such a suspended magnet stops spinning it will automatically align itself in a magnetic north/south direction just like the needle in a $1,000 surveyor's transit. Granted a transit can make accurate readings and precise sightings, but the fancy needle doesn't point to any truer north than the bar magnet.

Invisible lines of magnetic force extend between the North and South Poles running horizontally in relation to our position on the earth; when you hold a compass in your hand the needle responds to that force. Some compass manufacturers don't always stamp an *N* on the north-pointing end of the needle. They might indicate north by coloring one end of the needle red, or coloring the entire needle black with a white dot on the north-pointing end, or coloring it all red with a white dot!

North Isn't Always North

A compass needle doesn't always point exactly towards the North Pole. It can point to an area in Canada about 1,200

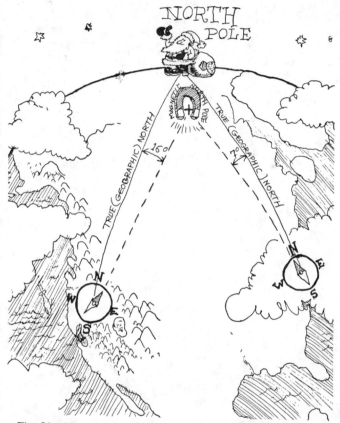

Fig. 38. The north of compass readings indicates magnetic north; this is not always the same as true north because the northern magnetic pole is about 1200 miles from the true geographic North Pole.

miles away from the North Pole. If you're in California, the needle will point to the right of true north. In Maine, the needle will point to the left. In Ontario, Michigan, Indiana, Kentucky, eastern Tennessee, South Carolina, and Venezuela the needle points to true north.

The difference between the direction of true north and the magnetic North Pole is called magnetic declination or magnetic deviation. Some orienteering courses try to teach you how to memorize whether the needle points to the right or the left of true north with rhymes about east being least and west being best, but they seem more confusing than helpful. Unless you're using a map with a compass, none of this will matter anyhow.

A map will usually have an arrow on it pointing to true north and a shorter arrow pointing to the right or left of the vertical arrow with the letters *MN* next to it. The shorter arrow indicates magnetic north, the direction the compass arrow will point in that particular area. Some maps have an even shorter third arrow with the letters *GN* (grid north) next to it. This grid system is rarely of any use to mountain travelers, but I know you're dying to find out what it means. Grid north is a tiny correction for the fact that the lines of longitude actually get closer as they approach the poles, while the grid patterns on the map are true squares. Surveyors and some military personnel use this system, but you shouldn't worry about it. Just concentrate on the MN arrow. Even using magnetic north as true north is sufficient if you're lost and too confused to figure out declination.

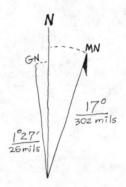

Fig. 39. The declination indicator on a map will show true north with a shorter arrow to the right or left indicating magnetic north and possibly an additional pointer for grid north.

What Type of Compass to Buy

The type of compass you buy depends on what you plan to use it for. Even a toy compass out of a Cracker Jack box will work just fine if all you want to do is find north, south, east, and west.

The simplest and least expensive compass contains a small magnetic needle teetering on a pivot at the midpoint, enclosed in some sort of housing. It will have a circular dial with the letters *N, E, S,* and *W* on it. Improved compasses are usually filled with liquid to reduce the number of oscillations the needle makes before it stops at a north/south position. Sometimes the number of degrees in a circle (0 to 360) appears on

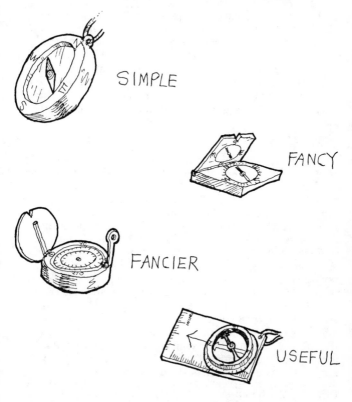

Fig. 40. Many types of compasses are available; all are usable for simple direction-finding. The most elaborate compasses have many features, but a sturdy serviceable model will be the most useful.

the compass. You can use the degrees to determine direction.
This is referred to as azimuth. It means that instead of east,
the direction is 90 degrees. Instead of west, it's 270 degrees,
and so on.

A more elaborate compass might have markings indicating
the 6400 mils or 400 grads into which a circle is divided in
more complex systems. It might also have a mirror or aperture
sight so you can take bearings, an adjustable base to correct
magnetic declination, and special metal housing to protect the
compass from being crushed.

The compass I find most useful for mountain navigation is a
plastic model with the housing mounted near one end of the
rectangular base plate and a direction-finding arrow etched on
the other end. Silva and Suunto are popular brands that come
in a variety of styles. I wouldn't advise buying a Cruiser or
Forester model because the east/west and 0–360 degree markings are reversed. It's easy to follow bearings with this compass, but it's hard to transfer them from the compass to the
map.

Trust Your Compass—It's Better at This Than You Are

The chances of power lines or lightning breaking your compass are small. But if you're near power lines or anything made
of iron like ice axes, knives, belt buckles, cameras, or steel-
rimmed glasses, the needle will be temporarily deflected. One
time I laid my map on the hood of the car, then put my compass on top of the map to orient it. The compass made no
sense at all because the iron in the hood was deflecting the
needle. Large iron ore deposits in certain parts of the country
can affect a compass needle, but those areas are rare. Maps
usually indicate their existence.

If it looks like your compass is going haywire, chances are
it's you who's off, not the compass. Twice on overcast days
after traveling cross-country for about half an hour I checked
my compass and was positive that the needle was pointing in
the wrong direction. After some head scratching and a little
meandering I figured out that *my* sense of direction was wrong,
not the compass. I'd been walking around in circles.

Orienting the Compass

To orient a compass merely turn it so the parts marked
north, south, east, and west actually align with the true north,
south, east, and west direction of the earth. Rotate the com-

pass housing until the letter *N* on the dial is in the same position relative to the north end of the needle as the true north and MN lines on the declination indicator (see illustration on this page).

By orienting a compass you can: (1) Determine cardinal points when you can use the borderline method of navigation, (2) orient your map, and (3) take bearings. All of these navigational techniques are discussed in the following paragraphs.

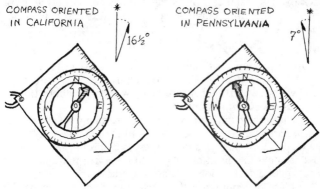

COMPASS ORIENTED IN CALIFORNIA 16½°

COMPASS ORIENTED IN PENNSYLVANIA 7°

Fig. 41. To orient your compass, rotate the compass housing until the letter *N* on the dial is in the same position relative to the north end of the needle as the north and MN lines are to each other on the declination indicator of your map.

The Borderline Method

The borderline method of navigating through the wilderness is so simple most people think, "Wait, this is too easy; give me something more complicated." But it's the best method I know. Dozens of times when I've been *temporarily* lost, the borderline method proved to be an efficient way of getting *unlost*.

If you were lost and knew enough about the area from a map or because you'd been in the general vicinity before, you could select a linear landmark (borderline) like a road or coastline, determine in which direction it is with your compass, and hike towards it. There's nothing complicated about that. As long as you know which end of the needle points north, you can figure out the rest. Since roads and coastlines are long, you won't have to worry about walking in a straight line towards your goal; the general direction will do.

Roads make the best borderlines. Trails aren't as reliable since you could cross one unknowingly if it happened to be covered with rocks or snow. Mountain roads are unmistakable even with ten feet of snow on them. Most North American mountain ranges run north/south, and the roads crossing them tend to run east/west. If you parked your car on one of these roads, then went hiking and got lost, all you'd have to know is if you were to the north or south of the road in order to get back to it. Streams and rivers can work as borderlines, but you might wander into a closer stream and mistake it for the one you really want.

Orienting the Map

Orienting a map is essentially the same as orienting a compass. You turn the map so north, east, south, and west correspond with the earth. There are many ways to go about this, but these two are the simplest:

1. Place the compass anywhere on the map with the north/south marks on the compass parallel to the north/south line on the map. Turn the map and compass as a unit until the compass needle is in a position relative to the north that matches the magnetic declination on that particular map.

2. Place the compass directly over the magnetic declination indicator on the border of the map. (Ignore all the numbers and letters on the housing unit in the compass.) Turn the map and compass as a unit until the needle is parallel to the MN arrow on the map. (It's not necessary to orient the compass with this method.)

Regardless of how you orient the map, the purpose is to position it so the printed features are in the same direction as the landscape.

Compass Bearings

Knowing how to shoot and plot compass bearings enables you to pinpoint your location. Even though the borderline method does the same thing and is less complicated, on two occasions this sophisticated technique really helped me out. One trip in particular involved an attempt to ski to the Clark Range of the Sierra Nevadas by following Illilouette Creek upstream to its source. Our party stayed out in what we optimistically hoped would be a brief storm, but it went on for three days. Finally the clouds lifted. Since we hadn't been able to identify any landmarks until then, we weren't sure how far up-stream we'd progressed. By taking a bearing on a distant peak and plotting it on the map, we discovered that we were further away from our goal than we thought. The storm started brew-ing again, so we gave up and went back.

One more story—this one's a little different. On a month-long ski tour across the massive ice fields and glaciers of the St. Elias Mountains in Alaska, the dimensions of the land were so gigantic that perspective was misleading. Even after a day of traveling, the peaks we could see at the edge of the ice field looked as though they hadn't changed position at all. How-ever, when we shot and plotted compass bearings on the peaks, we were able to confirm the fact that we'd made some progress. Our sense of walking on an icy treadmill was merely an illusion.

Now that you know how useful compass bearings can be, this is how to take and plot them. One technique in particular —resection or cross bearings—involves taking bearings on two known landmarks and plotting them on a map so the intersec-tion defines your location. Don't expect to be able to pinpoint your location any closer than by about a quarter mile with this method. The only drawback with this technique is that you need two landmarks.

To take a bearing you need to determine the angle between north and the line of sight to the landmark. Most compasses have devices like flip-up aperture sights, notches, mirrors, or direction-finding arrows that allow you to do this. To shoot a bearing accurately, face the landmark, aim the arrow or sight towards it, then orient the compass. Make sure the sight is still on the landmark while you orient the compass. Then read the bearing at the appropriate notch or marker. This is referred to as true bearing since it relates to a true geographic north/south line. (If you're using a military compass with a magnetized disk instead of a needle, you'll have to take a magnetic bearing which relates the angle between the line-of-sight and magnetic north.)

Once a bearing has been shot and you've determined the number of degrees between the landmark and true north, a rep-resentation of the bearing can be plotted on the map. If you have a protractor, use it to plot the bearing by drawing a line from the landmark at the angle of your bearing. However, the base plates or frames of many compasses are designed with a

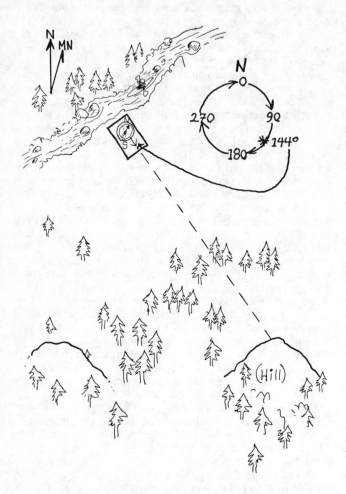

Fig. 42. In plotting your position on a map, first choose a visible landmark some distance away and use your compass to determine the angle between true north and the line of sight to the landmark.

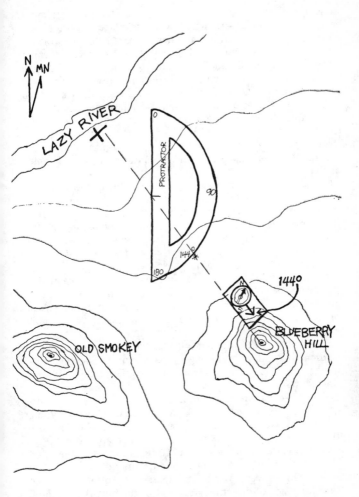

Fig. 43. To transfer the compass reading to the map, use a protractor to plot the angle of the bearing; then draw a line from the landmark at the angle of your bearing.

straight edge to use instead of a protractor. With the desired
bearing set at the direction-finding arrow, place the compass
on the map so the north/south lines are parallel to the north/
south lines on the compass. The angle of the direction-finding
arrow will then be the same as what a protractor would describe.
Since the compass is serving as a protractor now, it isn't always
essential that the map be oriented or the needle in any particular position. However, many maps don't have enough true
north/south lines printed on them for handy alignment with
the compass. So you might want to orient the map. Then if
the compass is also oriented, you can put it on the map and
the direction-finding arrow will automatically be at the angle
of the bearing.

Once you get the proper angle, draw a line at the angle
across the map from the landmark. Position the compass on
the map so both norths are parallel and the straight edge of
the compass is over the landmark. A line drawn along that
edge will indicate the line-of-sight from where the bearing was
taken. If you shoot the bearing from a known stream, ridge,
or trail, extend the line to that baseline to determine your
exact location. Don't draw the line in the exact opposite direction from the landmark, away from where you shot the bearing, because then the plotted line won't cross the trail, stream,
or ridge as it should. If the lines don't intersect, it's probably
because you plotted one or both lines in exactly the opposite
direction from the landmark. If your compass has a direction-
finding arrow, it will point away from you towards the landmark. As a result, the line from the landmark will be opposite
the arrow.

Try to select landmarks that are approximately ninety degrees apart for optimum accuracy. If you know where you are
and would like to identify a distant peak, take a bearing on
the peak and plot it from your site on the map in the direction
of the direction-finding arrow until the line crosses the peak on
the map. If you want to travel to a destination you can't see,
reverse this process. Use the compass as a protractor and measure the angle of direction (relative to true north) between the
starting point and the destination on the map. Follow the
bearing by sighting along the direction-finding arrow with the
oriented compass. Look past the sighting notches or arrow and
locate a distant landmark that happens to be in that line. Then
walk to the landmark and take another shot to locate another

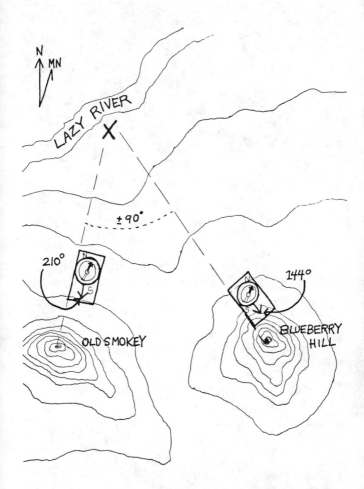

Fig. 44. Plot another bearing using a second landmark, preferably one about 90° to the right or left of the first landmark. Your location will be approximately where the two bearing lines cross on the map.

Fig. 45. The best way to learn to use a map is by practicing navigation in favorable, unhurried circumstances, preferably in a familiar area. (Note the stones being used to anchor the map.)

landmark. Repeat the process until you reach your destination.

In open country there may be miles between landmarks, in dense woods perhaps only a hundred feet. It's rarely necessary or practical to expend the energy it takes to follow precise bearings over hill and dale. Follow a bearing loosely along the path of least resistance towards a baseline.

MAP READING—LOOKS LIKE GREEK TO ME

At first glance a topographical map with all those funny marks, wiggly lines, and different colors leaves most people thoroughly confused. And understandably so. Just what does all that weird looking stuff mean? Well, you can find what kind of terrain lies ahead, where water can be found, high points, low points, paths, highways—all sorts of useful information that could save your life, keep you from getting lost, or prevent your stumbling into an unexpected gorge. At any rate, an understanding of maps and map jargon will certainly make your trip into the wilderness easier and more enjoyable.

You don't have to understand absolutely everything on a topographical map to get some good information from it. Certain marks and lines on these maps are easier to decipher than others. The best way to learn how to read a map is by actually getting out there with one, preferably in an area you're familiar with, and matching the map to the surrounding terrain. Try to do this if you can, but do take your time. Map reading can't be learned in one afternoon, but eventually everything will start to fall into place—the cliffs, rivers, gorges, hills.

Three types of maps can be easily obtained: highway maps from gas stations, Forest Service maps, and United States Geographical Society topographical maps (USGS topos, for short). The highway maps are probably the least reliable. They represent roads accurately, but peaks, streams, and ridges might be erroneously shown. U.S. Forest Service maps and USGS topos are better for off-road travel. Some local ranger stations will give you Forest Service maps free of charge—the last of the red-hot deals. These maps accurately represent roads, peaks, streams, trails, shelters, and springs. They are frequently more up-to-date than USGS topos, indicating highways, logging roads, and trails that didn't exist when the older topos were drawn. However, as Forest Service maps don't have contour

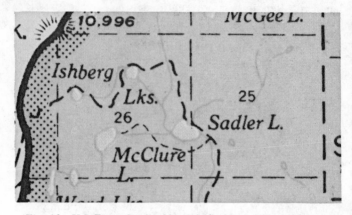

Fig. 46. U.S. Forest Service Map (1976). Note: (1) lack of contour lines to show terrain steepness, (2) presence of Public Land System section lines for sections 25 and 26, (3) trail (dashed line) between Sadler Lake and McClure Lake, which didn't exist when 1953 USGS topo map was made, and (4) lack of shading to differentiate forested from non-forested areas.

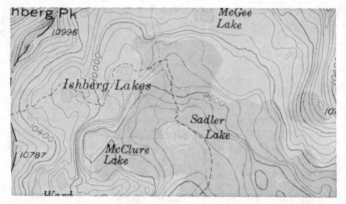

Fig. 47. USGS Topographical Map (1953). Note: (1) contour lines indicate steep terrain on the west (left) side of McClure Lake, (2) lack of section lines (many USGS topo maps do include section lines), (3) lack of trail between Sadler Lake and McClure Lake, and (4) shaded area indicates forest; unshaded area is rock or meadow.

lines, you can't tell if a stream plunges down a steep-walled gorge or flows gently across a broad valley. Since USGS topos do have contour lines, it's best to use them together with up-to-date Forest Service maps.

Some well-stocked bookstores sell USGS topos. If you can't find the map you want, write to the USGS (Denver, Colorado 80255 or Washington, D.C. 20242). They'll send you a free index of the topo maps available by state and an order blank with prices for different types of maps. If you know a few weeks ahead of time that you're going on a backcountry trip, try to order the map before you leave. Even if you don't know how to read it yet, you can learn by doing.

The most popular topo for the outdoor enthusiast is the fifteen-minute quadrangle, a rectangular map that represents an area covered by fifteen minutes of latitude and fifteen minutes of longitude—approximately ten miles by fifteen miles. A degree of latitude or longitude is divided into sixty minutes. For even finer designations a minute is subdivided into sixty seconds. One inch on a fifteen-minute quad usually represents 62,500 inches, approximately one mile. For even more detail you can use a seven-and-a-half-minute quad which includes one-fourth the area covered by a fifteen-minute quad expanded onto an even larger piece of paper. Less detailed but sometimes the only thing available is the 1:250,000 scale map. It covers two degrees of longitude and one degree of latitude.

How to Determine Mileage

If you want to know how many miles lie ahead, measure the straight line length of the map with a ruler, stick, pencil, or whatever. Then hold the measuring instrument next to the scale indicator on the bottom of the map to determine the actual distance in miles or kilometers. If the area you're measuring is hilly, increase the measured flat distance by ten or twenty percent to arrive at a fairly realistic mileage estimate. If you're measuring a winding river or trail, lay a piece of string along the route on the map, then pull the string straight and hold it against the scale indicator.

The red (sometimes black) vertical and horizontal section lines on the map can also be used to determine mileage. These lines were originally developed by the Public Land System to divide land for private ownership into basic square mile units (640 acres) called sections. These sections are grouped into blocks of thirty-six (six by six) called townships. Each township is uniquely defined by a horizontal range indicator (such as R24E) and vertically by a tier, or township, indicator (such as T1N). By counting the number of sections or of townships you plan to cross, you can quickly approximate the mileage. If you're traveling in national forests or parks, you might encounter metal tags nailed to trees with the exact location of the tree, in terms of the Public Land System (PLS), printed on the tag. Then you can determine your position by comparing the information on the tag with the PLS line on the map.

The Colors

Red or black colorations (including pink, purple, etc.) represent man-made features such as roads, trails, or buildings and boundary and grid lines. Green shading represents woodlands or forests which vary in density depending on the part of the country. Most North American mountain forests are open, shady areas that are pleasant for off-road travel. The forest in the Pacific Northwest, the Gulf and Atlantic coastlands, and the timberline growths in the Adirondack and White Mountains of the East are heavily overgrown with tangled underbrush. These areas are difficult to travel through unless you're following a path or wide stream bed.

White indicates treeless areas: rocks, sand, snow, or green meadows. A mottled green and white coloration indicates bushes, but since the map can't tell you what type of bushes, don't assume you can easily travel through them. They might be extremely thick.

With the exception of grid marks on the edge of maps, blue represents water. Thin blue lines indicate streams; blue shading signifies lakes and ponds. A thirsty hiker should look for a solid blue line because it means fairly permanent water. Fortunately, 80 per cent of the blue areas on mountain maps will have water even during dry periods. Some maps indicate permanent glaciers and snowfields with blue lines and outline the perimeter of the glacier with blue dashes. The contour lines inside the perimeter are also blue. Since certain portions of glaciers and snowpacks are always melting they provide water at high altitudes even during the driest part of the summer.

Contour lines on topographical maps are typically brown in color. Each line is drawn to represent the earth's surface at a specific elevation above sea level. If contour lines seem incomprehensible, and they do to many people, use a shaded relief contour map (available from the USGS for certain areas). These easily-understood maps show terrain features with brown shading that represent shadows as they might look from above during a summer sunset.

Contour lines are always drawn side-by-side. The space between them, which varies, represents degrees of elevation. On the bottom of fifteen-minute quads you'll usually see in capital letters *CONTOUR INTERVAL EIGHTY FEET*. That means that each contour line is eighty feet of elevation above or below the contour line next to it. Lots of white space between contour lines means you'll have to walk a long way to gain or lose eighty feet of elevation. When the lines are fairly close together, the terrain is steep and you'll only have to travel a short distance horizontally, to go up or down eighty feet. Lines with no space between them indicate very steep terrain that's best avoided. Maps with eighty-foot contour intervals won't give a clue to the existence of forty-foot-high cliffs that are impassable. So if you're hiking off-trail, allow enough time and plan alternate routes in case you run into one of these little surprises.

Up From Down

Distinguishing between uphill and downhill on topographical maps requires close attention to detail especially if the land's fairly level. The elevation is printed on some contour lines but the following tips should help you out.

1. When a series of adjacent contour lines form V's as they intersect a blue stream line, the apex of the V will point upstream.

2. A series of circular contour lines indicates mounds, hills, or peaks. The highest part will be in the center of the circle. A contour circle with short brown tick marks along the edge indicates a bowl or depression in the landscape.

Triangles, Plus Symbols, and X's

Some maps have rather strange-looking *X*'s on them with the letters *BM* and an elevation number, or sometimes you'll see small triangles with a dot in the middle. These symbols are called bench marks. If you went to the actual site of the *X* or

Fig. 48. A bench mark is a permanent metal marker stamped with the elevation at that location. Bench marks correspond to symbols on USGS topo maps.

triangle, you'd find a metal marker set permanently into the ground—on a pipe, concrete slab, or even a tree—with the elevation stamped on it. If you were lost and stumbled onto one of these bench marks, you could compare the elevation printed on the metal cap with the bench mark symbols on the map and pinpoint your location (assuming the bench mark was placed prior to the printing of the map).

Elevations printed in blue or brown on USGS topos are considered less precise than those printed in black. Sometimes the letters *VABM* (vertical angle bench mark) will appear instead of *BM*. That means that the elevation was calculated by a surveyor who sighted the spot, usually a mountain summit, from another already-known elevation rather than actually measuring it foot-by-foot from one point to another.

Don't confuse bench marks with the slightly larger plus symbols used to determine the specific latitude and longitude of any point on the map. If imaginary lines were followed horizontally and vertically from the plus symbol, they would intersect with the map edges at small (usually black) tick marks

next to the numbers indicating the minutes location of a particular geographic line.

Now For the Hard Part—Grid Systems

I saved the best for the last. All those tick marks on the side
of the map are part of a grid system. Military and rescue teams
rely on this system to communicate specific locations over the
phone or by radio in an emergency. Although you'll probably
never have to use the grid system, at least you'll know what
the marks mean. The following is the simplest explanation I
can give for a rather complex system. (If you decide to skip
this section, I'll understand.)

The thousand-meter grid which is also known as the Univer-
sal Transverse Mercator grid or the Military Grid Reference
System is the most commonly used method. The tick marks
on the edge of the map indicate imaginary vertical and horizontal lines across the earth at a spacing of one thousand
meters. The grid lines are numbered consecutively from arbi-
trarily chosen horizontal and vertical lines. Usually the equator
forms the horizontal base for these systems while various other
vertical zero lines are used. The digits indicating thousands
and tens of thousands of meters are printed in a larger type and
on a lower base than the digits that precede them. A typical
notation for a horizontal grid line would show a superscripted
43 followed by a larger (in type) two-digit number like 85. If
you follow the map border to one corner, you'll find a similar
number followed by "ooom.N." which identifies that particular grid line as 4,385,000 meters north of the equator! (Aren't
you glad you asked?) A vertical grid line might be shown as a
superscripted 2 followed by a larger 94 which means 294,000
meters from a vertical zero line. In the "Read Right Up" military method, only the large numbers are used with accuracy
to three or four places. In three-place accuracy, the intersec-
tion of these two lines would be given as 940850. Some maps
also include a 1,000-foot grid system which uses ordinary
numbers.

Both the grid system and the township method (mentioned
earlier) are used to communicate specific locations during
emergencies. However, what's usually said goes something
like "Down at the lake three miles northeast of Such-and-Such
Peak." If the person on the other end of the line is using a map

similar to yours, features in the printing can pinpoint a location. For instance, you can say "Near the *B* in Grizzly Bear National Park." To avoid mistakes, describe the location in terms of two independent systems: "The center of the northwest quarter of section 36, R23E, T2N, at the lake three miles northeast of Such-and-Such Peak."

Chapter Eight:
The Lost and Found Department

The first time I ever got lost was at the ripe old age of six. I was tagging along with my father and brother who were surveying boundary lines in the forest. Being closer to the ground and more into insects at the time than boundary lines, I stopped to watch a millipede earnestly making its way across a log. Fascinated by this creature's amazing mode of locomotion and all those legs, I stood there mesmerized. When I looked up everyone was gone. Deserted! All alone in the forest and I'm only six. My heart started pounding, I broke out into a cold sweat, and I felt sick to my stomach. After the initial shock of "Omigod, where is everyone?" it occurred to me to start yelling. Fortunately my father answered immediately. He and my brother were only about a hundred yards away but hidden by dense trees. Even though I was *officially* lost for only a few minutes, the sick feeling of dread that came over me was unforgettable. I've been more seriously lost since then and I always get that same sick feeling. Chances are you'll react the same way if lost. It's a perfectly normal reaction. Recognize it for that. However, the most important advice I can give you if lost is to try to remain calm. I know that's easier said than done, but it's almost impossible to think logically and get yourself out when your brain and body are consumed by panic.

TRAVELING IN PAIRS OR GROUPS

The chances of getting lost decrease tremendously if you travel with one or more friends since partners can correct each other's navigational mistakes. But it's easy to get separated, especially if your pace is different or you disagree on which routes to follow. At the beginning of your trip, emphasize how important it is to stay together; make a

Fig. 49. The chances of getting lost decrease tremendously if you travel with one or more friends, as partners can correct each other's navigational mistakes.

resolution to keep an eye on each other. This isn't any different from when you were a kid and you'd hear "Now stay together so you won't get lost." It made sense then and it still does.

GOING SOLO

I can't honestly condemn solo hiking or skiing since I do it myself. It's an extremely rewarding experience both physically and mentally—a great way to get away from it all and clear out the cobwebs. However, if you're traveling cross-country alone and break a leg you stand a good chance of dying out there. I'm not trying to scare anyone, but those are the facts. If you do go solo, *always* let someone (preferably a person who likes you) know where you're going and when you'll be back. Always carry plenty of emergency equipment so you can get yourself out of any trouble.

SO YOU'RE LOST—NOW WHAT DO YOU DO?

Let's assume that you've been on a day hike and are heading back towards the car. You keep hiking and hiking. Eventually it occurs to you that you should have reached the car an hour ago. You're not *that* worried. You're probably just a little lost. The car is bound to be right through those trees.

STOP. Under these circumstances most people have the urge to plunge ahead a few more feet, then yet a few more feet. The feet turn into yards, the yards into miles. Obviously you already made a mistake somewhere along the line. Going forward will only get you more lost.

Sit down. Relax. Take a fifteen-minute break and try to talk yourself out of any "what if I'm really lost and they never find me" feelings. Think back on where you might have gone wrong. Did you take the wrong fork in the path? Are the streams flowing in the wrong direction? If so, maybe you unknowingly crossed a divide into another watershed. Maybe you wound up on a deer path instead of a people path. Deer trails are only about nine inches wide and often have logs across them. Human trails are at least twice that size and obstacles like logs are usually cut or cleared away. Check out the path you've been following. Look at your map if you have one and reorient yourself. Remember, try to remain calm. Your goal is to get out of this situation. Panic only makes things worse. Thrashing around in the forest without any specific goal in

Fig. 50. A wider path and cut logs are two important ways to differentiate human trails from animal paths.

mind is like chasing your own tail. Go at it half-blind without a plan and you could end up traveling in circles. All sorts of things can be done to get you unlost.

Go Climb a Tree

You might be able to see familiar landmarks like your car or a road from the top of a tree, but don't climb one unless it's safe. You don't want to be lost and injured too. You could hike to a nearby high point of land for a view, a much safer (and easier) method than tree-climbing.

Backtracking

If there are obvious tracks left in the snow or soft soil, then backtracking is fairly easy. However, if the tracks are hard to follow, it will be difficult to retrace your steps. Also your route will probably appear much different as you look back on it. When you travel in unfamiliar territory, always glance back occasionally and memorize the landscape from the opposite perspective.

Fig. 51. Your route often appears unfamiliar when returning in the opposite direction. Look back occasionally as you travel and memorize what the route looks like from that perspective.

Along the Blazing Trail

Sometimes trails are marked with blazes so keep an eye out for them. They're diamond- or T-shaped sections of bark

Fig. 52. (left) Trails are sometimes marked with diamond- or T-shaped blazes chopped out of the bark of a tree.

Fig. 53. (right) A cairn or duck is a pyramid-shaped pile of rocks used to mark the trail in treeless areas.

chopped out from tree trunks usually four to ten feet above the ground. Older blazes may be barely distinguishable light scars on the trunk. In treeless areas trails are sometimes marked with cairns or ducks which are piles of rocks built up like pyramids.

Stretch Those Vocal Cords

A little yelling and shouting certainly can't hurt. Someone might be nearby and hear you. But don't be fooled by the spooks. You can hear them faintly when you're alone in the forest, especially if it's windy. Depending on your school of thought, these voices could be ghosts, the wind, or your vivid imagination. At any rate, they can't help you, so don't follow their illusive lead.

Don't Call—Just Whistle

Whistles work even better than vocal cords, and they don't consume as much energy. If you've strayed away from friends, blow long single blasts. If you really need help fast, blow the whistle three separate times with pauses in between. If traveling with a group, establish at the beginning of your trip the difference between "Hey, where are you guys?" and "Get help fast!" signals. Since kids can't shout as loud as adults (some parents might disagree) the whistles could come in handy.

TO STAY OR NOT TO STAY

If shouting, whistling, tree-climbing, and backtracking don't work, then you need to decide whether to stay and wait for help or try to get out on your own. Some experts recommend always staying since leaving might get you even more lost. But sometimes it's better to leave. Do so only if you're in good shape and can handle what could turn out to be a real endurance test, the terrain is safe to travel in, a *specific* course can be followed to a *specific* destination, and if it's safer to leave because of impending lightning, hypothermia, etc. If you're too tired to leave, stay and wait for rescue or rest and leave later. If you're a plane crash survivor, then stay if it's safe. A search party can spot a plane wreck easier than a lone person walking in the forest.

Whether you stay or leave, you might have to spend a couple of nights out. This shouldn't be a frightening experience as long as there are shelter materials around and you have some survival equipment with you. Give yourself at least two hours before it gets dark to locate a good sleeping site with a favorable microclimate and sufficient firewood.

The most important factor in weathering the situation is your own response. So remember, if lost:

1. Stop, sit down, calm down, think
2. Reorient yourself or backtrack
3. Shout or whistle
4. Either bivouac and wait for rescue or travel along a *known* course towards a *known* goal.

X MARKS THE SPOT

If you decide to stay and wait for rescue, there are various ways of signaling for help that can be seen or heard from far away. You've probably seen most of these methods in the movies—giant X's on the ground, smoke signals, three shots from a gun, reflector mirrors, etc. Any of these methods will attract attention assuming a search party is already looking for you. *Any* unnatural sign, even a bright shirt or sleeping bag hung in a clearing, will probably be investigated. Use your imagination.

Three of Anything

A pattern of three signals to indicate distress is universally recognized: three shots from a gun, three blinks from a flashlight, three blasts on a whistle, three fires burning at night. As long as it's three of something, chances are it will be checked out.

Make an X

A large ground symbol in an X-shape means "unable to proceed" to military aviators. But almost anyone, military or otherwise, recognizes an X as a sign for help. Even if your shelter is deep in the forest make an X in a large clearing. If you're in snow, use green pine boughs to make the X or stomp a trench in the snow so it casts a dark shadow. If you're in a green meadow, use logs bleached white by the sun or light-colored rocks. Make the X at least forty feet in length so it can be seen from the air.

Smoke Signals

A fairly large fire with lots of smoke can be seen from far away. If you're in a green forest with a dark blue sky overhead, add pine boughs, green vegetation, wet leaves, or moss to make the smoke white. It will contrast nicely against the sky. If you want black smoke to contrast against a background of snow, gray rocks, or clouds, add petroleum-based materials like car tires or motor oil, if available. If you can, build three fires far enough apart so the smoke rises in three separate columns. Remember, three of anything. . . .

Mirrors or Metal

A signal mirror is an excellent instrument for attracting
attention as long as the sun is bright, someone's around to see
it, and you know how to aim it. The famous case of the Andes
aircraft survivors of 1972 illustrates what can happen if you
don't know how to aim a signal mirror—nothing. On the third
day after their plane had crashed on a high mountain snowfield, four planes flew overhead. Since the white fuselage of
the broken plane was practically invisible from the air, the survivors tried to signal by reflecting the sun's rays against shiny
pieces of metal. But they didn't know how to aim the metal
and their efforts went unnoticed.

Signal mirrors you can buy will either have mirrors or shiny
metal on both sides and a hole in the middle. Aiming one is
pretty simple, but it sounds complicated if you only read the
instructions and don't actually do it. Go outside on a sunny
day and try aiming it at specific targets like rocks, fence posts,
or nosy neighbors. Face your target. Hold the mirror about a
foot or two away from your face and aim the hole at your target. Unless you're able to center the hole directly on the target, a ray of sunlight will come through the hole and land on
your face. You'll see that "sunspot" on your face when you
look in the side of the mirror facing you. Tilt the mirror slowly, this way and that, until the sunspot disappears, that is, when
it's centered in the hole. At this point, with the sunspot centered in the hole and the target visible through the hole, the
sunlight striking the other side of the mirror will reflect directly on the target. Your aim is perfect!

Like I said, it sounds complicated, but it really isn't. Once
you actually use the mirror you'll see what I'm talking about.
But it's a good idea to learn how to aim it at home rather than
in an emergency situation.

Signal mirrors can signal a target on any horizon, even one
opposite the sun. If the mirror has a polished surface you can
signal ten to fifteen miles on a bright day. It's even possible to
signal a commercial jet airliner 40,000 feet in the air. Try to
deliver a three-flash signal to the pilot who can relay the distress
message to an airport which will contact the proper authorities.

Ordinary glass mirrors like those found in some compasses
aren't as accurate as signal mirrors, but if that's all you have,
give it a try. To aim the mirror, extend one arm, fingertips up,

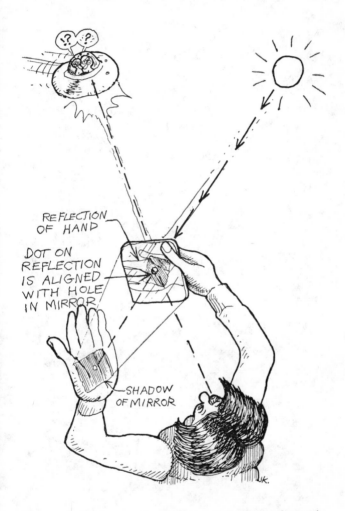

REFLECTION OF HAND

DOT ON REFLECTION IS ALIGNED WITH HOLE IN MIRROR

SHADOW OF MIRROR

Fig. 54. Buy and carry a signal mirror or improvise one from a tin can lid. It must be shiny on both sides and have a hole in the middle. Learn how to use it *before* you need it in an emergency situation.

Then reflect first on finger tips then on aircraft

sight aircraft over fingertips →

Fig. 55. An ordinary glass mirror can also be used as a signal mirror.

and look over your fingers at the target. Now hold the mirror in the other hand in front of your face, tilting it until the sunlight is reflected onto the fingertips of your extended arm. At this point, tilt the mirror up a little so the reflection passes over your fingertips and onto the target. This isn't a highly accurate method, but it's better than nothing.

SURVIVAL KITS

The only problem with survival kits is the risk of putting all your eggs into one basket: drop the basket and all the eggs get broken. Leave the kit at home and it does no good if you're stranded. My solution is to keep a mental list of survival items in order of priority. Then as the possibility of needing them increases, I carry more of the items on the list.

If you're going on a day hike in a meadow, you probably only need to carry the first few items on your list. If you're going on a long hike or ski tour, you should probably carry all of the items. You can buy a survival kit or make one from a coffee can. If you're carrying backpacking equipment, you don't really need a special kit. Let's look at some survival items in order of priority and their special uses.

Fig. 56. A suggested minimal survival kit: matches in a waterproof container, compass, whistle, pocketknife, and lightweight Space Blanket.

Dry Matches

These are of top priority to a person stranded in the wilderness. Windproof matches and the so-called waterproof matches get wet from the inside if water wicks up the wooden stem to the powder. Carry them either in a waterproof container, well-wrapped in Saran Wrap, or inside a plastic sandwich bag. If there isn't a surface to strike the match on, use the metal zipper on your pants (carefully!). Wooden matches are easier to strike than paper matches, but book matches are more compact and less expensive. By packing them in sandwich bags, I can store quite a few in pockets, day packs, or camera bags.

Pocketknife

You'll get a lot of use from a pocketknife whether in a survival situation, camping, or just picnicking. You can gouge holes in leather or wood, cut guy lines to size, slice this, whittle that, and so on. Some people prefer large hunting knives. Others like the smaller but more versatile gadget pocketknives that include screwdrivers, can and bottle openers, awls, corkscrews, saws, scissors, toothpicks, tweezers, spoons, whittles, and (if you can find it) a knifeblade Even a little penknife can be helpful in an emergency.

A Wool Shirt or Sweater

Although these items aren't norn ally included on survival lists, they're sometimes more useful than survival kits. Stash a pack of matches and some dimes in one pocket to add versatility.

Plastic Garbage Bag

If bad weather is unlikely and you can't see lugging around a raincoat or poncho, stuff a folded plastic garbage bag into your shirt pocket or day pack. The bag can be used as a poncho by cutting holes for your face and arms, and then pulling it over your head. Cut along one side and the bottom and use as a waterproof ground cover or roof. Or use it to collect water dripping from rocks and icicles.

Wire

You can repair equipment with wire, snare animals (use 28 gauge piano wire for small game), or suspend a cook pot from

Fig. 57. A plastic garbage bag is a versatile emergency item, serving as a poncho, groundcover, or water collector.

a branch over the fire so it doesn't have to rest unsteadily on firewood.

Salt Tablets

To help replace the salt lost from perspiring during a day of heavy exertion, thus relieving fatigue and warding off muscle cramps, take salt tablets. Drink at least one cup of water with the tablets or they'll make you nauseous. You can also make a salty broth with them by adding bouillon cubes and water.

Tea Bags

Although there's nothing nutritional about it, tea is nice to have on a bivouac to flavor the otherwise flat-tasting hot water you drink to stay warm. If you don't have any tea bags, steep fresh pine needles in hot water for flavor and a vitamin C bonus.

Ski Repair Equipment

Carry repair equipment if you're touring far into the woods and don't want to walk back. Sometimes the bail (toe clamp) on your light touring bindings will fly off during a fall and disappear into the snow. If you don't have an extra bail, your ski is useless. Either carry a replacement bail or tie a six-inch piece of string or wire between the bail and the binding. Then even if the bail pops, it will stay attached to the piece of string or wire and can be reinstalled.

Binding screws can tear out and get lost—carry spares. Pack the enlarged hole where the screw came out with steel wool to keep the replacement screw firmly in place.

The Packrat Method

No one wants to carry a twenty-pound survival kit around. Try to make mini-survival kits from the clothes and equipment you normally carry. Instead of taking a corkscrew, use a gadget pocketknife with *everything* on it. An angler's creel or a camera hunter's equipment bag can hold a few emergency items. Drill a hole in the butt of a hunting rifle and stuff it with a small toy whistle, some matches, a dime, and fishhooks.

Survival Equipment List

In order of priority:

Matches, waterproof or in a
  waterproof container
Dime and/or quarter to call for
  help from a pay phone
Pocketknife
Compass
Whistle
Space Blanket
Wool shirt or sweater
Map
Plastic garbage bag, raincoat,
  or poncho
Food
Adhesive tape
Nylon cord (parachute cord),
  at least fifty feet
Candle stub for firestarting
Wire
Tin can or pot for cooking,
  melting snow, digging, etc.

Water purification tablets
Insect repellent
Salt tablets
Signal mirror
Fish hooks, dry flies, nylon
  leader, lead sinkers
Flashlight or penlight
Sewing needle and thread
Pencil
Safety pins

Additional emergency items
for cross-country skiers:

Spare ski tip (if using wooden skis)
Extra cable or extra bail for
  bindings
Screwdriver
Extra screws
Steel wool to tighten loose screws

Note: First-aid equipment hasn't been included because of the wide
      variation in individual medical competency and needs. A doctor
      may carry narcotics, syringes, and bulb catheters, while someone
      else may be satisfied with a few band-aids and aspirin.

Epilogue

After reading this book, you might think the mountains are human deathtraps, where blizzards occur on cue and every other trail leads to quicksand. Really, who but a hard-core masochist would voluntarily expose himself to altitude sickness, hypothermia, frostbite, and animal attack? Who but a stoic fanatic would sleep with nothing more than a thin pad between his body and the hard, cold ground, or choose a powder snow shelter over a warm motel room? "Not me," you say. "You'll never catch me crawling around those cold mountains!"

Hopefully I haven't completely scared you into the comfort of that warm hotel room over the mountains. Even though hazards exist in the mountains, if you can identify them and act appropriately, your backcountry experience will be tremendously rewarding both mentally and physically.

If you're a beginner, start out with short excursions. Learn how to identify local plants, animals, rocks, and weather patterns. Learn how to interact with the natural environment without destroying it so others can enjoy the same experience. Then gradually and safely extend your excursions deeper into the mountains. Or as John Muir so eloquently expressed it:

Climb the mountains and get their good tidings.

Nature's peace will flow into you as sunshine flows into trees.

The winds will blow their freshness into you, and the storms their energy, while care will drop away from you like the leaves in autumn.

Appendix

Winter Camping Equipment

Despite the weather's snowing and blowing, winter camping can be comfortable *if* you've got the right equipment. A malfunctioning stove, a broken shoulder strap, or wet socks could create a disaster if you're not properly equipped. The following list describes the type of equipment you should carry to insure safety *and* comfort.

Pack: A winter backpack should be larger than a summer pack, obviously, because of the extra clothes and equipment you'll have to carry. If your present pack isn't large enough, buy some removable side pockets to increase capacity and carry several straps or short lengths of cord to tie gear on the outside of the pack.

Tubular aluminum frame packs are good for winter camping, but skiers may find that the frame interferes with a complete poling motion. Soft or frameless packs such as the Ultima Thule are excellent for skiers because they keep the pack weight close to the body. Unfortunately they require careful arrangement of items inside and most are slightly small for winter camping. Internal frame packs can be packed fast, but they are somewhat unwieldy for skiers. The Lowe Alpine Systems expedition pack is one of the largest capacity internal frame packs and has one of the most comfortable waist belts available.

Most packs can be adjusted to fit your body. Read the adjustment instructions that come with the pack or go to a reputable dealer to have it fitted.

Tent: Unless you are staying in the same place for several nights, carrying a tent is more practical than building a snow shelter. There is an overwhelming array of good tents available. A Gore-Tex tent is lightweight, but a nylon tent with rain-fly will be warmer and much less expensive. Choose one with a waterproof floor and treat the floor seams with sealer. A zippered cookhole may be a source of leaks, but in winter it will expedite cooking and cleaning inside the tent. Remember: always have adequate ventilation (no heavy winds, just some moving fresh air) when cooking or using a lantern inside a tent.

Sponge: For sopping water off the tent floor if your waterproof fabric and sealer fail you.

Sleeping bag: It should have a minimum of three inches* of dead air insulation on top of the sleeper. Bags filled with synthetics such as Polarguard and Fiberfill II will weigh about 30 per cent more than down bags but only cost half as much. For one-night trips, down bags are most practical. For longer winter trips, when morning frost accumulates in the bag, a synthetic-fill outer bag or all synthetic-fill bag will be heavier but more useful than all down, which drops tremendously in insulating value when wet.

Bag length should be long enough for you, your boots, and a hot water bottle to warm your feet.

Foam pad: If you're camping on snow, you'll want a thicker pad than you'd use in summer. A ½"-thick ensolite or 1½"-thick open-cell foam pad (sheathed in waterproof material) will suffice for most campers. Get a full-length pad or use a half-length pad with software (clothing, pack) under your legs, feet, and head.

Ground cloth: Use a waterproof cloth to protect your sleeping bag from tracked-in snow and dirt. A poncho can also serve as a ground cloth.

Stove: Melting snow into water for a group demands a stove with a large flame and high volume fuel tank. Svea and Primus 71L stoves are poor in these respects. The larger Optimus 8R and 111B stoves, the MSR stove, the Coleman Peak 1, and the Phoebus 625 are excellent winter stoves. The Phoebus and Coleman stoves are the quietest—a boon when you're cooking and talking inside a tent (well-ventilated, remember). Butane stoves (Bleuet, Primus, Gerry) burn poorly when the air temperature is low or when the fuel cannister is less than one-third full.

Ensolite pad, small: Cut the pad to fit the bottom of your stove so the stove won't sink as its heat melts the snow beneath it.

Fuel bottles: Aluminum Sigg bottles are excellent (replace washers periodically). Many polyethylene bottles will hold gas without dissolving or leaking, but give yours a trial run at home before the trip. Before putting the fuel bottle in your pack, test for leaks by turning the bottle upside-down, then shaking or squeezing it. Carry fuel bottles in outside pack pockets where leaks won't contaminate food. Allow at least 8 ounces of white gas per person per day when snow camping.

Pots and utensils: carry one pot for melting snow and one or two others for cooking. A nesting set is most practical. Remember handles for cook pots, a large metal or unbreakable plastic spoon, and a soft plastic cup or bowl that won't crack when crushed in a pack or when hot food is added in cold weather.

Plastic water bottle: This is the easiest and safest way to carry water; a wide-mouthed bottle facilitates adding snow or your favorite electrolyte powder (ERG, Gatorade, Wylers, etc.)

Food: The simplicity of preparing instant and freeze-dried foods makes them convenient for snow camping. They are available in supermarkets and mountaineering supply houses. Carry lots of high energy trail snacks and an extra day's ration in case you run into more trouble than you were expecting.

Breakfast is the most difficult meal to make simple, palatable, and nutritious. A hot drink with your favorite dried fruit, nuts, and granola is one way to start the day out well.

Sugar consumption is high on winter trips; carry some extra to add to hot drinks and cereal. Honey is more nutritious, but stiff and uncooperative when cold. Halvah, nutritional yeast, and protein powder are less publicized but excellent winter camping foods.

Scouring pad and paper towels: Dishes can be washed without soap by using boiling water, a scouring pad to scrub off burned-on foods, and paper towels.

Clothing: It's actually easier to stay warm when traveling in the Arctic than in the Sierra; Arctic temperatures are so low that snow doesn't melt on or dampen clothing. Conversely, the relatively warm Sierran winter temperatures quickly make clothes damp from the snow, thus reducing insulating value. Don't let mild temperatures fool you into dressing improperly.

Wet wool clothing is warmer than other wet clothing. Synthetics (Polarguard, polyester pile) are lighter than wool and dry faster. Down is lightest in weight but useless when wet and slow to dry.

At night, put damp clothes inside a plastic bag in your sleeping bag to keep them from freezing. (The plastic bag will prevent the dampness from migrating into your sleeping bag fill.) Alternatively, place damp clothes over you between your inner and outer bag, if you're able to dry the bag in the morning.

Storm clothing: Wear a cagoule, poncho, or rainchaps and jacket made of waterproof nylon, foamback, or Gore-Tex materials. 60/40 material is poor protection from rain or wet snow. A zippered front and ventilation openings under the armpits will help prevent overheating.

Headgear: Wear a wool balaclava (knit cap with pull-down face and neck protection).

Snow goggles: For extremely cold, windy conditions, usually above timberline, double-lens air barrier goggles are best. Also use an anti-fog cloth, stick, or liquid on the lenses.

Underwear: Wet cotton underwear saps heat from your body. Wool underwear irritates sensitive skins and won't wick perspiration away from the skin very well. Either carry spare dry cotton underwear or use a thin layer of 50/50 cotton-polyester which wicks well and dries suitably fast.

Sweater, jacket, vest: These are best if made from wool, polyester pile, or down as discussed above.

Gloves: Carry extra gloves. Cotton or leather-palmed gloves are rugged for dry days. Use wool gloves in foul weather. Mitts are warmer than gloves. Use overmitts of Gore-Tex or nylon for severely cold weather.

Pants: Nylon ski knickers shed snow well and are appropriate for warm Sierra winter days. Wear wool knickers in colder weather. During very severe weather, add breathable synthetic powder pants, snowmobile pants, or wind pants that are designed so you can put them on while wearing boots.

Gaiters: They keep your calves warm and keep snow out of your boots. Breathable gaiters are normally preferable to waterproof because they allow body moisture to escape. However, during winter rainstorms, waterproof gaiters will be superior.

Socks: Wool-synthetic blends combine wet warmth with durability. A thin pair of cotton or synthetic socks next to the skin will alleviate the wool itchies. Wear enough socks to fill your boots comfortably. A crammed-in foot will be colder due to decreased circulation.

Boots: They don't have to be big and heavy to be warm. A thick combination of socks and insulated overboots with a light boot is just as effective as a double mountaineering boot. Seal the boots to keep water out. Change your socks often to keep feet dry, warm, and blister-free.

Overboots: These are an oft-neglected item of importance. Several designs and brands are available, from homemade cut-up ragg-wool socks to pull-over touring booties to Supergaitors.

Sun protection: Take an extra pair of sunglasses on long trips. Sun creams containing PABA work well at Sierran altitudes if applied liberally and frequently on skin exposed to the sun. Zinc oxide is effective but messy. A tennis visor will protect your nose on spring tours.

Miscellaneous: Toilet paper; toothbrush; plastic trash bags (use for ground cloth, pack cover, or trash); matches in waterproof container; candles to light your tent or snow cave; map and compass; Chapstick or Blistex; appropriate ski waxes, scrapers, torches; 100 feet of light nylon line (bears may be around even in winter); wrist or pocket watch so you know how much daylight is left.

Optional: Avalanche cord, though unless you're conducting an avalanche rescue, you shouldn't be in terrain where you need one. Pocket radio transceivers have proven to be more reliable but are expensive. Snow shovel, saw, smoke flare, flare gun (unlikely to be used on routine trips), camera, radio.

Glossary

altitude sickness general term for any of a variety of illnesses caused by slow acclimatization to rapid increase in altitude; includes Cerebral Edema (CE), High Altitude Pulmonary Edema (HAPE), and acute mountain sickness

azimuth distance in angular degrees from the north point (in the Northern hemisphere) in a clockwise direction

balaclava knit cap with visor, face opening, and neck extension

bench mark surveyor's mark made on a landmark of known altitude and position

blaze diamond- or T-shaped mark made on a tree to mark a trail; usually made four to six feet above ground

cagoule pullover raincoat with hood

cairn pyramid-shaped pile of stones built as a landmark or trail marker

closed-cell foam very dense foam rubber for use under sleeping bag; will not soak up water

conduction transmission of heat by contact of a warm object with a colder one

convection transference of heat from a warm object to a less warm one by movement of a fluid substance; here used to mean the effect of wind

duck same as *cairn*

evaporation heat loss occurring when water is changed into vapor

frostbite the freezing of body tissue caused by exposure to intense cold

frostnip less severe or superficial frostbite

grid systems a series of consecutively numbered, intersecting horizontal and vertical lines on a map. Specific locations can be designated by the number of horizontal and vertical grid lines that cross a particular area

hypothermia subnormal body temperature occurring when the body loses heat faster than it can replace it; also called exposure

loft thickness of sleeping bag (used here as one layer of thickness, that is, top or bottom layer)

magnetic declination angle of the difference between a line pointing to true north and one pointing to the magnetic North Pole

plus symbol map mark indicating specific latitude and longitude of any point on that map

priming getting a stove going by first pouring and burning a small amount of fuel

radiation sending out or radiating heat from a warm object to a less warm one

snow blindness painful but temporary blindness from over-exposure to snow-reflected ultraviolet rays; a sunburn of the cornea

tarn small mountain lake or alpine pond

true bearing angle formed by true north and viewer's line of sight

Bibliography

Angier, Bradford, *Field Guide to Edible Wild Plants*. Harrisburg, Pennsylvania: Stackpole Books, 1974.
Good illustrations of many plant species found throughout North America.

Burt, Calvin P. and Heyl, Frank G., *Edible and Poisonous Plants of the Western States*. Lake Oswego, Oregon: By authors, n.d.
Playing card format with excellent photos.

Cunningham, Gerry, *How to Keep Warm*. 1972. Available by writing author, Division of Outdoor Sports Industries, Inc., 5450 North Valley Highway, Denver, CO 80216.
An enlightening if brief (15 pages) pamphlet explaining theoretical principles of dressing for warmth.

Davis, Adelle, *Let's Eat Right to Keep Fit*. New York: Harcourt Brace Jovanovich, 1970.
Well-informed conclusions about human nutrition; Davis often differs from official government information on nutrition and diet.

Fletcher, Colin, *The New Complete Walker*. New York, Knopf, 1974.
Enjoyable reading with much pertinent information for the backpacker.

James, Wilma Roberts, *Know Your Poisonous Plants*. Healdsburg, California: Naturegraph Press, 1973.

La Chapelle, Edward, *The ABC of Avalanche Safety*. 1970. Available from Division of Outdoor Sports Industries, Inc., 5450 North Valley Highway, Denver, CO 80216.
Clearly written booklet providing valuable technical information.

Lathrop, Theodore G., M.D., *Hypothermia, Killer of the Unprepared*. Portland, Oregon: The Mazamas, 1970.

Lloyd, E., "Airway Warming in Accidental Hypothermia,"
Mountain Medicine and Physiology. London: Alpine Club,
1975.

Mountain Medicine Symposium, Proceedings. Yosemite, California: Yosemite Institute, 1976. Available from The Yosemite Institute, Yosemite National Park, Yosemite, CA 95389.
Explicit descriptions of current mountain medical termin-
ology, especially in treatment of hypothermia and altitude
sickness.

Mountaineering, the Freedom of the Hills. Seattle, Washington:
Mountaineers, 1974. Available by writing Mountaineers,
P.O. Box 122, Seattle, WA 98101.
This is the most comprehensive available text about moun-
tain excursions.

Shires, G. Tomas, M.D., *Care of the Trauma Patient*. New
York: McGraw-Hill, 1966.

Tejada-Flores, Lito and Steck, Allen, *Wilderness Skiing*. San
Francisco: Sierra Club Books, 1972.
Aside from the poor Nordic technique section, this is a
valuable treatise on wilderness skiing; see especially the
chapter on snow and avalanches.

Thompson, Steven and Mary,/*Wild Food Plants of the Sierra*.
Berkeley, California: Wilderness Press, 1976.
An environmentally conscious book with much practical
information about edible plants. The descriptive text more
than compensates for the weak illustrations.

United States Department of Agriculture, *Food: The Yearbook
of Agriculture,* Washington, D.C.: Government Printing
Office, 1959.
The government's conclusions about human nutrition.

Washburn, Bradford, *Frostbite*. New York: American Alpine
Club, 1962.
The original and excellent treatise on modern methods of
frostbite diagnosis and treatment.

Watt, Bernice and Merrill, Annabel, *Composition of Foods*.
Washington, D.C.: Government Printing Office, 1963.

Wilkerson, James, M.D., *Medicine for Mountaineering*. Seattle,
Washington: Mountaineers, 1977. Available from Mountaineers, P.O. Box 122, Seattle, WA 98101.
The best text yet on dealing with medical problems in remote country.

Index

About the Author

Craig E. Patterson's first brush with wilderness—getting lost in the woods at age six—was just the beginning of his long association with the outdoors. As author, lecturer, and instructor, he has brought both the beauty and the rigors of the wilds to many eager explorers. Graduated from Penn State University, Patterson has worked as a petroleum engineer, mountain guide, emergency medical technician, and cross-country skiing, rock-climbing, and survival instructor. He is presently a Yosemite National Park ranger active in emergency medicine and search and rescue.